HOW TO BE A MORE SUCCESSFUL LANGUAGE LEARNER

Joan Rubin
&
Irene Thompson

HH

75204

Heinle & Heinle Publishers, Inc.
Boston, Massachusetts

P
51
R6

To our parents—
Ann and David, and Elena

Manufactured in the United States of America.

ISBN 0-8384-1124-X

10 9 8 7 6 5 4 3 2 1
85 84 83 82

Cover photograph: by Owen Franken from Stock, Boston.

Preface

If you are presently studying a foreign language or are planning to do so, this book is written for you. In it you will find concrete suggestions to help you become a more effective and successful language learner. You will also become acquainted with a host of time- and classroom-tested techniques that will enable you to approach the study of a foreign language in a meaningful and productive way—to derive from your study of a language what *you personally* want from it.

In today's world, contact with speakers of languages other than English is increasingly common; we encounter such people in school, in our travels, in our jobs. As these contacts increase, so does our motivation to study foreign languages. For many the study of a foreign language is a satisfying and truly rewarding experience. Others, however, consider it a frustrating, nearly impossible undertaking. We believe that you can avoid inclusion in the second group if you take the time to learn and understand some basic facts about yourself, about language and communication, and about the way in which languages are learned. We also believe that *now* is the time to do it!

Our purpose in writing this book, therefore, is to share with you, in nontechnical terms, the kinds of insights that will enable you to become a better foreign-language learner. We examine such questions as:

- Why study a foreign language?
- What characterizes a good language learner?
- What is the nature of language and communication?
- Where is a language best learned?
- How does one begin to master a foreign language?

With your help, we also examine you! That is, we ask you to consider what *you* bring to the language-learning process: *your* specific abilities, *your* personality, *your* personal goals, *your* motivation, *your* attitudes. In short, what we do is provide you with the means to become the kind of foreign language learner *you* want to be.

Contents

Preface   iii

PART 1   ABOUT LANGUAGE AND LANGUAGE LEARNING   1

Chapter 1   You, the Language Learner   3
Chapter 2   Clarifying Objectives   13
Chapter 3   Instructional Settings   23
Chapter 4   The Communication Process   27
Chapter 5   The Nature of Language   41

PART 2   HOW TO BE A BETTER LANGUAGE LEARNER: LEARNING STRATEGIES   47

Strategy 1   Find Your Own Way   49
Strategy 2   Organize   53
Strategy 3   Be Creative   57
Strategy 4   Make Your Own Opportunities   61
Strategy 5   Learn to Live with Uncertainty   65
Strategy 6   Use Mnemonics   67
Strategy 7   Make Errors Work   69
Strategy 8   Use Your Linguistic Knowledge   73
Strategy 9   Let Context Help You   75
Strategy 10   Learn to Make Intelligent Guesses   77
Strategy 11   Learn Some Lines as Wholes   79
Strategy 12   Learn Formalized Routines   81

Strategy 13   Learn Production Techniques   85
Strategy 14   Use Different Styles of Speech   89

PART 3   AIDS FOR THE LANGUAGE LEARNER   93
Language Teachers   95
Language Textbooks   97
Dictionaries   99
Language Tapes and Recordings   101
Reference Grammars   103
The Wider World   105
Selecting the Language Course
That's Right for You   107

ABOUT THE AUTHORS   111

Forewords

I was pleased to have the chance to go through the manuscript of *How to Be a More Successful Language Learner*.

Unfortunately in the United States today we are not learning foreign languages as we should, and there has developed even a fear of learning foreign languages. There is a surprising attitude that Americans are somehow less able to learn foreign languages than people in other countries. That is, of course, a myth, but a widely held myth. And it is a myth that this book helps to destroy. Any student who follows the advice of this book will be a better language student.

I applaud this endeavor, and my only regret is that I didn't have an opportunity to read a book like this before I became a language student during my college days.

The Honorable Paul Simon
House of Representatives
Congress of the United States

I am happy to write an endorsement of Joan Rubin's and Irene Thompson's book *How to Be a More Successful Language Learner*, which clearly meets a need we in the profession have felt for a long time and have attempted to answer in various ways. This new book can take its place alongside Moulton's *Linguistic Guide to Language Learning* and is, moreover, shorter, handier, and more explicitly aimed at the student than was its predecessor.

In my view, foreign language professionals have no worthier mission in life than to teach our students that all languages (and all cultures) are equal and are equally valid ways of organizing experience. A basic point, yet subtle enough to require explicit attention. The point is masterfully made by Rubin and Thompson. Their organization is clear, the examples well chosen, the material neither too heavy nor too light.

Not surprisingly, some teachers are still poorly informed and uncertain about linguistics. They will benefit from reading this book on their own. They will then, I predict, be eager to share its insightful perceptions with their students.

Richard I. Brod—Director, Foreign Language Programs, Modern Language Association of America

Reading the manuscript of *How to Be a More Successful Language Learner* by Joan Rubin and Irene Thompson has been a most exciting experience for me. Although the book addresses the language learner, there is no question that it is a valuable resource for the teacher as well. The book deals with many complex issues of language learning with sparkling clarity. The most recent discoveries in language acquisition research are explained in a manner easily understood by even the most uninitiated layperson. Pycholinguistics, sociolinguistics, the Sapir-Whorf hypothesis, nondefensive learning, learner-centered learning, multidisciplinary approaches, the socio-affective filter, acculturation, the psychodynamic monitor, creative construction, humanistic classroom, individual learning styles, learner needs, pragmatics, caretaker language, formulaic expressions—all these form the basis of the book. In addition, the proficiency ratings of the Department of State's Foreign Service Institute are very clearly described. Whereas many books confuse the reader, this book communicates.

In short, *How to Be a More Successful Language Learner* is a superb book, suitable for learner and teacher alike. It is a book that should be distributed as widely as possible, as rapidly as possible. The book is also timely in view of the findings of the President's Commission on Foreign Language and International Studies. It adds impetus to our realization of the increasing need for foreign language competence in an interdependent world. It will contribute to the solution of our pressing problems in the teaching and learning of foreign languages, as well as in the teaching of English to speakers of other languages. Domestically, it will contribute to the furthering of equal educational opportunities for people of all ages and walks of life. Internationally, it will contribute to cross-cultural understanding in the interest of world peace. I strongly recommend the book to faculty and students alike.

Professor James E. Alatis—Dean, School of Languages and Linguistics, Georgetown University, and Executive Director, Teachers of English to Speakers of other Languages (TESOL)

Part 1

ABOUT LANGUAGE AND LANGUAGE LEARNING

Chapter 1

YOU, THE LANGUAGE LEARNER

You, the language learner, are the most important factor in the language-learning process. Success or failure will, in the end, be determined by what you yourself contribute. Many

Everything depends on you.

learners tend to blame teachers, circumstances, and teaching materials for their lack of success, when the most important reasons for their success or failure can ultimately be found in themselves. There are several learner traits that are relevant to learning a foreign language, and they usually appear in combination. A *positive combination* of these traits is probably more important than any one alone.

It is important to realize that there is no stereotype of "the good language learner." There are, instead, many individual traits that contribute to success, and there are also many individual ways of learning a foreign language. People can compensate for the absence of one trait by relying more heavily on another, by accentuating their strengths to compensate for their weaknesses. There is no conclusive evidence that any one of the traits described below is more important than another, particularly over long periods of language study. The descriptions in this chapter are intended to help you analyze your predispositions. You will then better understand how to enhance your learning by accentuating your strengths and minimizing the effects of your weaknesses.

AGE AND FOREIGN-LANGUAGE LEARNING

Some people think that the best time to begin studying a foreign language is in childhood, and that the younger you are, the easier it **Children are** is to learn another language. There is little evidence, **not better** however, that children in language classrooms learn **learners.** foreign languages any better than adults (people over age 15) in similar classroom situations. In fact, adults have many advantages over children: better memories, more efficient ways of organizing information, longer attention spans, better study habits, and greater ability to handle complex mental tasks. Adults are often better motivated than children: they see learning a foreign language as necessary for education or career. In addition, adults are particularly sensitive to correctness of grammar and appropriateness of vocabulary, two factors that receive much attention in most language classrooms.

Age does have some disadvantages, however. For instance, adults usually want to learn a foreign language in a hurry, unlike children, who can devote more time to language mastery. Also, adults have complex communication needs that extend beyond the mere ability to carry on a simple conversation. Adults need to be able to argue, persuade, express concern, object, explain, and present information about complex matters that pertain to their work or education. Because most adults do not like to appear foolish, they often deny themselves opportunities to practice for fear of making mistakes, not getting their message across, or appearing ridiculously incompetent. Also adults have more trouble than children in making new friends who speak the foreign language.

One example usually given to support the notion of children's superiority as language learners is their ability to pick up an authentic accent. It is usually observed that children of immigrants learn to speak the language of their adopted country without an accent, whereas their parents rarely do. It is also observed that even adults with high need and motivation, such as diplomats, rarely learn a foreign language without retaining some of their native accent. In a sense, the same is true in sports: to learn well the complex coordination of the hundreds of muscles needed to play tennis, swim, or figure skate, a person has to start young. Most champions begin training at an early age. There are examples of strong competitors who entered their sport after childhood, but they are the exception, not the rule. The same is true of adults who acquire native-like accents.

Taken together, the disadvantages of age are clearly offset by advantages. By properly combining positive traits and effective strategies, you *can* indeed master a foreign language—as lots of adults do.

The best time to learn a foreign language, then, is when your need is clearest and you have sufficient time. If you are strongly motivated to study a foreign language and if you have the time to do it, the best time to begin is *now*.

INTELLECTUAL PREDISPOSITIONS

A person's intellectual predisposition to learn a foreign language is commonly referred to as *aptitude*. Aptitude is another way of saying "knack for languages," and like "having a good ear for languages," it is one of those myths people use to explain why some succeed where others fail. Strictly speaking, language-learning aptitude is the intellectual capacity to learn a foreign language, a kind of a foreign language IQ. In a classroom situation, a person with high language aptitude can usually master foreign language material faster and better than someone with lower aptitude. Thus, several studies show a strong relationship between grades and aptitude.

What is your language IQ? There are several standardized tests that measure language-learning aptitude. They predict how fast and how well an individual can learn foreign languages under formal classroom conditions, when the emphasis is on *grammar* and *memorization*. However, these tests may not be such good predictors of how well a person can learn to *communicate* in a foreign language, especially if he or she has the opportunity to practice in real-life situations. In other words, language aptitude tests may predict ability to learn formally and analytically, but they may not be as reliable in measuring ability to learn unconsciously and intuitively.

Remember that language success may ultimately depend not only on ability but on persistence. You may have the potential to be a brilliant language learner, but if you fail to put effort into it, chances are you will not learn much. A good combination of talent and perseverance is ideal. For example, it has been shown that pronunciation accuracy in adult students can be predicted by two traits: aptitude for mimicry, presumably an inherent trait, and strength of concern for pronunciation, a motivational factor. When the two are combined, one can acquire a good foreign accent.

PSYCHOLOGICAL PREDISPOSITIONS

A number of psychological traits appear to be related to successful language learning. One of them, motivation, is so important that it is discussed separately in Chapter 2. In this chapter we examine several other traits that have a significant effect on language mastery.

Attitude

If aptitude is an intellectual trait, attitude is an emotional one. On the one hand, it may have to do with the way learners feel about

Emotions are important.

the foreign culture and its people. They may admire them and want to learn more about them by becoming fluent in their language. Or, they may like the people who speak the foreign language and wish to be accepted by them. Research has shown a definite relationship between attitudes and success when foreign-language learners have an opportunity to know people who speak the language they are studying. Such positive attitudes usually help learners to maintain their interest long enough to achieve language mastery. Thus, if you find France and the French people attractive, if you wish to learn more about them or wish to become more like them, you are likely to succeed at learning to speak French well.

Some people are remarkably successful in mastering a language without feeling powerfully drawn to the country or the people who speak it. They may need the language for academic or career purposes, so their attitude is purely pragmatic. These two attitudes are not mutually exclusive: it is entirely possible that a person may want to learn Spanish because he or she wants to understand the Spanish people better *and* wants to study in Spain. More important than specific attitude is that the language learner experience a real need to communicate and make meanings clear.

Extroversion

It should not be surprising that personality influences the way a person goes about learning a foreign language. Although we can-

Practice is important.

not, at present, sketch the ideal language-learning personality, several traits appear to be related to success. Of these, extroversion is repeatedly mentioned as a positive trait. When everything else is equal, a sociable person who uses every opportunity to talk with other people may be more successful because by initiating and maintaining more contacts he or she has more occasion to hear and use the new language.

Inhibition

People who are painfully aware of their limitations and worry about their ability to use the language are usually less willing to engage in either classroom practice or in real-world communication. Shyness and inhibition can stand in the way of progress in speaking (perhaps less in the way of reading) a foreign language. They can also prevent a person from taking risks or seizing opportunities to practice and learn. Fear of making a mistake or being misunderstood can keep a learner from adopting an open-minded, active, and creative approach to language learning. Everything else being equal, a person who has an open, receptive attitude towards the foreign language, who is not afraid to use it, and who feels at ease in foreign-language situations is more likely to learn from his or her language experiences.

Make yourself comfortable.

Thus, if you have an open, inquisitive, worry-free approach to learning a foreign language, if you find the whole experience enjoyable and rewarding, you will probably learn better. You may want to review your life situation in general and ask yourself the following questions: Is my self-esteem low in language class? If so, what can I do to raise it? (If your teacher is highly intolerant of errors, you may find it helpful, when you can, to change teachers.) Is there anything wrong with my study habits? Do I expect too much of myself? Do I really have the time to devote to language learning, or do I have too many other pressing matters on my mind?

Tolerance of Ambiguity

Tolerance of ambiguity allows a person to reconcile and accommodate ideas that may be contradictory or information that may be inconsistent. A person who is tolerant of ambiguity does not see everything in terms of black and white and does not put information in air-tight compartments. Such a person is willing to accept the fact that there are many shades of grey and that uncertainty and inconsistency must be accommodated. Tolerance of ambiguity has been noted as an asset in learning a foreign language because there are so many

Everything is not black and white.

inconsistencies in language rules that even native speakers cannot always agree on correct usage or explain certain language phenomena. Also, whether a turn of speech is right or wrong may depend on the situation rather than on an ironclad rule. A person who can accept an evasive answer, such as, "Well, I suppose you could say it that way under certain circumstances," is more likely to have an open, flexible system for accommodating new information as knowledge of the language increases.

Learning Style

Learning a foreign language is just one form of learning in general; therefore, each individual will employ the approach that he or she

Rules or risks? usually applies to other learning situations. When it comes to foreign languages, one kind of learner prefers a highly structured approach with much explanation in the mother tongue, graded exercises, constant correction, and careful formulation of rules. This type of learner is very analytical, reflective, and reluctant to say anything in the foreign language that is not grammatically perfect. This person is a rule learner. A second type of learner relies more on intuition, the gathering of examples, and imitation. He or she is willing to take risks. There is no evidence that one type of learner is more successful than the other. What is more important perhaps is that the learner's style be appropriate to the particular task. If the task is to communicate, then risk taking is in order. If the task is to say or write something correctly, then rules should be consulted.

It is important that each learner's preferences be accommodated in the classroom. You may thus wish to examine your own preferences, and communicate them to your teachers. For instance, if you feel that you need rules, you may be quite uncomfortable in a classroom dedicated to imitation and repetition of dialogues and should ask the teacher for more explanations. If, on the other hand, you feel that you learn more from being exposed to the language and from making your own inferences, you may feel ill-at-ease in a classroom where the teacher painstakingly explains the new grammar in English and should ask the teacher for more practice in speaking.

Eye-Ear Learning

When learning a foreign language, some students depend on their eyes; others depend on their ears. Some learners feel that they learn better if they can see the language written out, while others prefer to listen to tapes and records. It is not clear to what extent "eye-mindedness" and "ear-mindedness" are related to foreign-language mastery. You may want to experiment to find out whether a single method or a combination of the two works best for you.

SOCIOCULTURAL PREDISPOSITIONS

Language and culture are inseparably interwoven, so you cannot really learn one without learning something about the other. When you set out to study another language, you also set out to study the culture that gives it life and meaning. Your relationship to the people and their culture is directly relevant to your learning of their language. Let us look at this relationship more closely.

Stereotypes

Stereotypes are overgeneralizations, or caricatures, of other people. They can interfere with learning how to understand and communi-

Are you a cartoonist?

cate with members of other cultures. In a sense, they are defense mechanisms—a way of making the unknown more predictable. The Japanese are "inscrutable," the Russians are "boorish," the French are "snooty," the Arabs are "volatile and unstable." Such oversimplifications impair our objectivity because we then see only those aspects of a foreign culture that we wish to see—that is, the ones that fit the stereotype. Thus, an act of generosity by a Scotsman can be either overlooked or treated as an exception, and an American Peace Corps volunteer may be seen by nationals of the host-country as either a materialist or a misfit.

Once formed, stereotypes are difficult to dispel. But if you realize that your view of Spaniards, Frenchmen, Germans, or Italians is stereotyped, you should examine your views and try to become more objective and open-minded. You will find that there is a difference between a caricature and a real person. It is difficult to learn to communicate with a caricature; you can only do it with a real person.

Ethnocentrism

Ethnocentrism is closely related to reliance on stereotypes. It is the tendency to measure other people against one's own cultural yard-

The grass is always greener on my side. stick. Most of us believe that our way of life is the best and most natural one. Thus, when we encounter a different culture, we tend to judge it in terms of our own. Almost invariably, we feel that our culture is superior simply because we feel more comfortable with it and because it gives us a sense of security. Here are a few examples:

Americans like to separate work and private life; Latin Americans socialize a lot with their colleagues. Judged by the Latin American standard, Americans are cold and distant; judged from the American point of view, Latins don't know where to draw the line between work and play. Both feel uncomfortable with each other. This may inhibit the formation of meaningful relationships that would allow members of one group to learn the language and culture of the other.

Similarly, Americans like to pride themselves on their openness, their "telling it like it is." In the Middle East, such candor is seen not as a virtue, but as stupidity or obtuseness. A Middle Easterner uses involved circumlocutions to avoid stating what may be troubling or offensive to a listener. As a result, Americans feel that they cannot believe much of what Middle Easterners may tell them, while Middle Easterners perceive Americans as lacking in finesse. This, of course, can prevent both groups from having personal relationships that would allow them to learn each other's languages and customs.

PAST EXPERIENCES

Previous experiences with foreign-language study may influence future attempts. If, on the one hand, a person has had a favorable

Is there a foreign language in your past? experience studying one language and believes that he or she learned something valuable, that person will be predisposed to study another language and will approach it expecting to achieve success. On the other hand, if an individual's first experiences with a foreign language were not particularly pleasant or successful, he or she will tend to expect the next language-learning experience to be just as stressful and unfruitful as the first. Such a person should examine the reasons for the earlier lack of success. Perhaps it was due to a teacher that the learner did not like, a textbook that was not particularly helpful, a method that clashed with the learner's learning preferences, or perhaps it was due to the learner's own inexperience, absence of motivation, or lack of good reasons for studying the particular language. Chances are that these conditions will not be repeated or can be avoided the second time around. The best approach then is simply to wipe the slate clean and approach the study of the next language as a completely new experience.

Keep in mind, too, that people get better at whatever they do over a long period of time. In other words, based on past experience, they *learn how to learn*. People who have learned several languages usually report that each became successively easier to master, particularly if the languages were related. So don't be surprised when the star performer in your class tells you that it is his or her third or even fourth foreign language.

Chapter 2

CLARIFYING OBJECTIVES

OBJECTIVES FOR FOREIGN-LANGUAGE STUDY

There are many reasons for learning a foreign language, and there is no doubt that having a good one firmly in mind will enhance your chances for success. Most people need strong motiva-

Why study a foreign language? tion to complete the complex task of mastering a foreign language. Generally this motivation falls into one of the following categories:

- *Professional* Sometimes a person needs to learn a foreign language in connection with his or her job. Communicating in a foreign language is an integral part of the work of foreign service officers, interpreters, foreign language teachers, international business executives, and many other professionals.

- *Educational* Frequently a person needs to learn a foreign language in order to satisfy an educational requirement imposed by a school, college, or university, or to use materials published in another language.

- *Social* People such as foreign-based military personnel and their dependents, travelers, and those living in ethnically mixed urban areas often want to learn a foreign language in order to communicate on a primarily social level with speakers of the language.

- *Personal* Often people want to learn a foreign language for personal enrichment, to satisfy personal curiosity about a country and its culture, to find a fulfilling hobby, or to seek their own roots.

Of course, these reasons are not mutually exclusive, but usually complement each other: A person may *need* to learn a foreign language in connection with a job, but may also *enjoy* studying foreign languages for their own sake.

SETTING OBJECTIVES

Your chances for successfully learning a foreign language are further enhanced if you take charge of the situation; that is, if *you* deter-

Set your own objectives.

mine what *you* want to learn. This will help you select a foreign-language program, if you have not already done so, or help your clarify the program that you are already in. Having objectives firmly in mind will also help you select suitable materials, recordings, and activities. For instance, while your teacher's objective may be to teach the 15 lessons in your textbook, your personal objective may be to learn to communicate with native speakers about simple everyday matters. Unless the classroom objectives are filtered through your personal ones, they will remain simply lessons in the book, hours spent in class, and pages of written exercises that do not seem to apply to real life.

The extent to which you pursue your own objectives and adapt the objectives of the teacher or the course to your own may determine your ultimate success. Thus, you should translate the immediate objective of "I must learn the dialogue 'At the Post Office'" into your own objective: "I should be able to transact business at a foreign post office."

Such self-determination can be easily exercised in the case of pronunciation. You can decide whether it is important for you to have good pronunciation in a foreign language and allocate your efforts accordingly. For example, if you are going to use the language almost exclusively for reading, it is not important for you to have a good accent, even though your teacher may stress pronunciation in class.

Keep in mind, however, that your objectives may change as your level of mastery grows, both because previously difficult objectives may seem more attainable and because changes in your work, lifestyle, geography, or attitude may occur.

Keeping Objectives Realistic

As in all complex and longterm enterprises, your chances for success in language learning are vastly improved if you set realistic goals that can be attained in the time available. People often approach the study of a foreign language with nothing more than a vague "I want to learn Russian (French, German)" to guide them. Since this goal is not specific enough, they often expect to be able to understand, speak, read, and write a foreign language after a relatively short period of study. When they find themselves unable to communicate with native speakers about themselves, their work, or current events, unable to write a friendly note or business letter, or unable to read a newspaper article or follow a radio broadcast, they often become disillusioned and blame themselves, the teacher, the program, or the textbook for the lack of success. They may discontinue their study of the foreign language altogether, at the same time acquiring a negative attitude toward foreign-language study in general.

Such negative outcomes can be avoided when students realize that language learning entails a series of stages of achievement from the simple to the more complex, and that success at each stage requires a certain amount of practice in each of the skills of speaking, reading, listening, and writing. A learner should thus aspire to achievement stage by stage and to measure his or her success accordingly. By setting more modest, realistic objectives for yourself along the way, you can sustain more easily your motivation and interest.

When setting objectives, it is important to be realistic about the degree of your commitment and the amount of time you are able and willing to devote to language study. For instance, if you intend to spend two years in college studying a foreign language, it is realistic to expect to attain a minimum level of speaking proficiency and to be able to read simple prose in a commonly taught Western European language, such as Spanish, Italian, or French. It is unrealistic to expect to understand rapid native speech and foreign radio broadcasts, or to discuss current events and professional interests with native speakers.

You can't do everything at once. Learners often expect to be able to understand, speak, read, and write a foreign language even though they have had experience with only one or two of these activities. It is important to realize that although there is a lot of carry-over from one activity to another, each needs separate attention and practice in order to develop. For instance, if your study of a foreign language stresses reading and translating, it is doubtful that you will be readily able to understand native speakers or speak the language yourself. Conversely, if your language experience stresses speaking and understanding, you may not be able to write an essay. It is more probable, however, that you will be able to read the language particularly if it is related to yours. The point is that one must decide whether one needs all skills, some combination of them, or just one.

One of the main reasons for setting a goal, then, is that it will help you to choose activities that are important to you and prompt you to spend less time and effort on those that do not achieve your purposes.

SPEAKING OBJECTIVES

Suppose your reason for studying a foreign language is to learn to speak it. Since learning to speak is a complex skill, you should set step-by-step objectives for youself. As mentioned previously, these objectives should be reasonable, given the amount of time you have available.

How well do you want to speak? In order to think of speaking ability in terms of stages, it might be useful to adopt the system currently being used by the Foreign Service Institute of the U.S. Department of State and by the Educational Testing Service, a publisher of standardized tests. The system is used to measure the speaking ability of persons, regardless of how, where, or for how long they have studied a foreign language. The definition of each proficiency level is applicable to any language, although the amount of time to reach a given level varies widely from the so-called "easier" languages, such as Spanish and French, to the "most difficult" ones, such as Arabic or Japanese. These ratings are called S-ratings (S stands for speaking). They range from zero (no speaking proficiency at all) to 5 (speaking proficiency equal to that of an educated native speaker). All levels can be modified by a +. For our purposes, it is most useful to discuss the more central ratings, namely 1, 2, 3, and 4.

S-1/Survival

Suppose you want to take a trip to another country and would like to be able to survive on your own using that country's language. You need to be able to get a room in a hotel, tell a taxi driver where you want to go, order a meal in a restaurant, handle a simple shopping situation, ask for directions, and give basic information about yourself, such as your name, age, address, occupation, and the like. You should also be able to address people appropriately and to thank them when necessary. Normally people at this level have limited grammar and vocabulary, speak hesitantly in short or incomplete sentences, and make all sorts of mistakes in pronunciation, vocabulary, and grammar. They are usually incapable of a sustained conversation.

If this level will satisfy your needs as you define them, then learning words, prefabricated patterns, and conversational devices will probably help you more than learning about grammar. Learning a few formula sentences, such as *Could you tell me. . .?*, *Where is. . .?*, *What is this called?*, will be more useful than knowing case endings or irregular verb conjugations.

S-2/Limited Working Proficiency

Now let us assume that you need to know how to speak a foreign language in your work, but only in a limited way. Without going into details, you may need to describe your job and the organization you work for. You may have to handle simple job-related inquiries, direct people to the right office, answer the telephone, and handle other simple matters in the foreign language. At this point, you may also want to be able to converse with native speakers on a limited number of topics, mostly concerning yourself and your personal life.

To achieve this level, you need more grammar, more vocabulary, and greater fluency than for S-1. At S-2, people still make a number of mistakes and grope for words and expressions, but they are usually able to carry on limited conversations.

If this is your goal, you should make sure that your training includes some specific work-related learning materials and simulations of situations in which you may actually have to use the foreign language. You should also try to meet native speakers to practice conversing about simple personal subjects.

S-3/Professional Proficiency

If you have a very strong interest in the language and the country in which it is spoken and if you need the language to carry out fully the responsibilities of your job, you may aspire to a greater mastery of the spoken language than so far described. You may wish to be able to participate fully in conversations with native speakers on a variety of topics, including professional ones, with relative fluency and ease. At this point, you will need to have mastered most of the major grammatical features of the language and enough vocabulary to cover a large number of topics. Chances are that you will still make occasional mistakes or look for the right word or expression, but this should not affect your fluency too much.

Should the attainment of such a level of proficiency be your goal, you will have to study the language for an extended period of time. Experience shows that this is usually the highest level of spoken proficiency attained by persons who have studied the language formally without having had an opportunity to live in the country or in a community where it is spoken.

If you can reach this level of mastery, you can become a full participant in any communicative situation involving the foreign language. You have arrived, so to speak. Congratulations!

S-4/Distinguished Proficiency

If your aspirations are really high and you wish to be able to speak the foreign language almost like a native speaker, with a great degree of fluency, grammatical accuracy, and precision of vocabulary, you will need quite a few years of study and an extended stay in a country where the language is spoken. As a rule, very few learners can attain such a high level. But it is a goal to be aspired to if one is ambitious enough.

You can see now that people move from one level to the next as they continue their study of a foreign language. If you can identify the level you want to or need to achieve, you will be better able to focus your efforts. You will also feel more positive about your achievements because they will become more visible to you.

READING OBJECTIVES

Like speaking, reading can be thought of in terms of levels of difficulty. Depending upon your desires and needs, you may aim for one of the following levels of reading proficiency that are used by the Foreign Service Institute to measure the reading skills of foreign-service and other U.S. government personnel. These levels are called R-levels (R for reading).

R-1/Elementary Proficiency

At this level, a person can read only the simplest prose containing the most common words and grammatical constructions. Heavy re-

What do you want to read? liance on a dictionary is normal. Chances are you will not be able to read material much more difficult than the lessons in your book. In Western European languages that are highly similar to English, such as Spanish and French, this level is achieved in a relatively short time and usually forges ahead of speaking ability. In languages with different scripts, such as Arabic or Chinese, the situation can be reversed, and it can take a bit longer to learn to read things than to say them.

R-2/Limited Working Proficiency

At this stage, a person can read uncomplicated but authentic prose that treats familiar topics and contains many common words and familiar sentence patterns. Frequent use of the dictionary is necessary. You might be able to read simple stories and perhaps even short articles in newspapers and magazines. Anything more complicated would mean more frequent reliance on the dictionary. It is a good idea at this point to ask your teacher to recommend a simplified reader and to start looking at foreign language newspapers and magazines to see what you can pick out.

R-3/Professional Proficiency

At this level, a person can grasp the essentials of standard but uncomplicated prose, such as newspaper articles addressed to the general reader, routine, job-related correspondence, and technical material in your own special field, without a dictionary. If you are aiming at this level, you should make sure that you familiarize yourself with most of the special terms and expressions used in your particular field, be it linguistics, foreign affairs, or electronics. You will find that the more familiar you are with the topic at hand and the more key terms you know, the easier it is to grasp the essentials of your reading material. It is a good idea to invest in a quality dictionary at this point.

R-4/Full Proficiency

At this level, you can read anything published in the foreign language without a dictionary. If you want to be able to read as quickly and effortlessly in a foreign language as you can read in your native language, you must read as much in one as you do in the other. A very large vocabulary is the key that ultimately unlocks this level.

UNDERSTANDING OBJECTIVES

As with the other language skills, goals for understanding may be flexible. For instance, if your goal is to understand what native

Conversation or lecture?

speakers say in conversations, you should aim at creating opportunities for participation with native speakers. If your goal is to understand foreign radio broadcasts, you need to listen to the radio and to watch TV programs.

In general, however, the goals of listening comprehension are inextricably tied to the goals of speaking, so that the two usually develop more or less simultaneously. It is widely observed that listening comprehension in most cases outstrips speaking ability at all levels of proficiency. This means that you should not be surprised if you find that you can understand more than you can say yourself.

The ability to understand short sentences, as in conversations, does not automatically lead to the ability to follow a lecture or other extended presentation in a foreign language. If you need to follow lectures, you should include in your preparation attending talks and lectures in the foreign language or listening to taped presentations on different topics. You may want to start with familiar topics and then branch out as your familiarity with the language increases.

WRITING OBJECTIVES

Should your plans also include learning to write in the foreign language, you should be clear about what you will be writing. Writing

Personal note or essay?

short personal notes to friends is not the same as writing business letters, reports, or longer essays. Sophisticated prose requires more knowledge of vocabulary, syntax, and style than does personal correspondence.

It is a good idea to set goals for writing in the same way you set goals for other language skills. For instance, learn how to write personal letters to friends, then try your hand at composing a business letter.

The problem with writing is that even in your own language you need some help and instruction. Most people formally study writing their native language throughout their education. It is, therefore, a good idea to take some writing courses in a foreign language as well. It is a skill that requires much practice and feedback.

Chapter 3

INSTRUCTIONAL SETTINGS

There are two basic environments in which a language can be learned: formal and informal. When a language is learned mainly in a classroom or through audio-visual means, we often call this foreign language learning, whereas when it is learned in an informal setting, it is commonly referred to as second language learning.

INFORMAL SETTINGS

In an informal environment, that is, outside of the classroom or the language laboratory, communication is not generally organized around the learner's needs. It is not simplified, graded, or repetitive. An informal environment does, however, offer a great deal of information about the nature of interaction and about appropriate ways of speaking. It usually also offers clues to the meaning of a conversation, since the setting, the relationship between participants, and the topic are generally clear. Further, and more important, it offers one of the strongest reasons for learning—the need to communicate. Most people learn a language in order to talk to other people. In informal environments in which the listeners speak only the foreign language, the need to make oneself understood is crucial. Hence, informal environments offer unlimited opportunities for practice as well as instant reward—being understood. Punishment is just as instant and obvious—one fails to communicate.

The biggest classroom is the community.

In informal settings, learners are neither particularly aware that they are learning nor able to describe what they have learned. Since the primary use of language in informal settings is communication, persons learning another language in such settings usually go through a number of stages before attaining mastery. In the early stages they make lots of mistakes and rely heavily on their first language. With additional practice, they begin to make fewer mistakes and rely less on their native tongue. Eventually, they may reach a stage at which their speech approximates that of native speakers. Often learners in informal settings go through a silent period; they just listen to the new language and do not speak until they feel ready.

FORMAL SETTINGS

In formal environments, learning materials are generally graded, simplified, and arranged around specific linguistic structures and

The classroom is safe. vocabulary lists. This situation provides an opportunity to learn in progression, although the progression may have little to do with the learner's real-life language needs. The teacher usually provides feedback by correcting mistakes and emphasizing rules. Often the mother tongue is used for explanation and communication between teacher and students about everything not contained in the lesson.

Formal classroom environments do not, as a rule, offer strong motivation to communicate or the opportunity to observe the way language is used in real life. The emphasis is on knowing *about* the language, on being able to produce correct sentences on cue, and knowing why they are correct or incorrect. In the classroom, when a student speaks, he or she usually concentrates on producing correct grammar, with the content of the message often quite irrelevant. After all, when one is practicing the plural forms of nouns, it is relatively unimportant whether one pluralizes vegetables or pieces of furniture as long as one does so correctly. The focus is not on *what* is expressed but on *how* it is expressed. In real-world settings, however, confusing the endings on nouns is much less serious than confusing *vegetables* with *furniture*, or asking for *chairs* instead of *cherries*.

In formal settings, people usually first learn a structure and then try to practice it in different contexts. Once the "structure of the day" is mastered, the teacher proceeds to the next, until the students have completed a list of structures considered essential. There is no guarantee, however, that they will be able to use these structures when they need to convey a message and are concentrating on its meaning.

COMBINING FORMAL AND INFORMAL SETTINGS

Foreign-language educators argue about which is more beneficial for adult learners: studying a foreign language in the classroom or

Combine the best of the two worlds. using it in real-life situations. The answer to this question is that both are needed.

When beginning foreign-language learners study in the classroom without a chance for real-life interaction with native speakers, their only sources of input are the teacher, the textbook, and language tapes. They benefit from error correction, explanation of rules, and graded practice, which reduce information overload and provide a certain amount of security. The instructor often makes a conscious attempt to use simplified and familiar language, and this makes the students feel good. As the knowledge of the language increases, however, such study becomes less valuable than the use of the language outside the classroom.

An intermediate or advanced student usually profits more from a stay in the country where the language is spoken than from continuing classroom study. At the advanced level, it is more profitable to use the language as a tool to study other subjects: literature, politics, history, culture, and the like.

Both settings may also be helpful at the same time. Since most adults are more comfortable in structured situations yet also need the motivation to communicate that comes from informal settings, they should try to take advantage of both environments.

Chapter 4

THE COMMUNICATION PROCESS

ABOUT COMMUNICATION

As you think about your goals in studying a foreign language, many possible answers will come to mind: to learn the grammar or pronunciation, to have a good vocabulary, or to be able to speak correctly. While all of these are useful goals, we want to emphasize that for most people, the main goal of studying a foreign language is to be able to communicate. The essence of communication is sending and receiving messages effectively and negotiating meaning. If you want to learn another language quickly and efficiently, you should keep this main goal in mind, for the others will follow naturally.

The message is paramount.

We all learn our first language quite naturally by focusing on this need to communicate. We learn how to send and receive messages in an effective way in order to accomplish our social goals.

All native speakers communicate without thinking about the process. However, in order to speed up learning another language, it is helpful to become more aware of the knowledge and skills we bring to the process. By identifying and recognizing what we already know, we can more effectively guide our learning. We may be able to take shortcuts or recognize where we have gone wrong in expressing ourselves or in interpreting others' messages.

Two Kinds of Messages

Many people mistakenly think that language learning entails learning to translate word for word from the native to the new language.

Those who hold this basic misunderstanding of the communication process will find language learning next to impossible!

Behind this belief is the idea that sending messages is just a matter of supplying information about something the speaker knows or wants. This type of learner thinks that the task is to find the exact words that express this knowledge or desire in another language.

Language variation is important. The fact is that we can say the same thing in many different ways. For example, if we wanted a window closed, we could say so directly by giving a command: "Close the window!" Or, we could do so less strongly by asking, "Would you please close the window?" However, under other circumstances, we might choose to be quite indirect by saying, "I feel cold," or "It's cold in here." The way we choose to make this request would depend on to whom we are talking, how important the request may be, and how we feel that day. The point is that at the same time that we share information about our knowledge or desires we also send vital social messages. The two occur together inseparably in a language. It is next to impossible to send the one kind of message without the other.

There are very few situations in which referential meaning is paramount and little variation is tolerated. An exceptional example of this is the exchange that takes place between an air traffic controller and a pilot. In this case, variation is not possible and basic information exchange is of the essence. On the other hand, sometimes we use language only for social purposes with little exchange of information. For example, when English speakers ask "How are you?", they don't really want to know the answer in detail. Most of the time, we send both referential and social messages at one and the same time, with the social side being somewhat more important.

There is much more to language differences than mere differences in pronunciation, grammar, vocabulary, and expression. Communication is governed by rules that specify such things as who can participate, what the social relationships are, what subjects can be discussed, who initiates the conversation, how turns are taken, who chooses the form of address, and so forth.

Here is an example of how word-for-word translation might mislead us and how focusing only on referential meaning might cause us to miss the real message of a communication. In many parts of the world it is not polite to accept an offer of more food the first time it is offered. Americans may be surprised or annoyed that their polite "no, thank you" brings yet another offer of food. When native English speakers say no to offers of food, they really mean no. However, when translated into another language in another social setting, saying no to an offer of food may be interpreted as a polite refusal with anticipation that the real refusal will be made after the second or third offer. In fact, in many parts of the world, people are reluctant to appear too greedy or childlike by accepting food or drink the first or second time it is offered. On the other hand, foreign visitors to the United States may be disappointed when their polite "no, thank you" does *not* bring a second or third offer of food. The point is that although a form may permit translation, its social meaning (positive or negative) depends on customary use and on the associated social values within a particular social context.

Finding the *appropriate* expression to use and paying attention to the *way* something is expressed are important because they are part of the messages people send and receive. Through the *form* we use, we express our feelings about a person or situation. For example, consider the distinction many languages make between the formal and familiar forms for "you" and "thou." With just a change of pronoun form, you can express contempt or respect, friendship or indifference. Further, knowing when to switch from "you" to "thou," and who may initiate the switch, is essential. Premature use of "thou" can nip a budding friendship or, if intentionally employed, be a deadly insult. On the other hand, failure to shift from formal to familiar at the right moment can be read as indifference or stuffiness.

It is usually more important to find the *appropriate* way of expressing yourself than to be grammatically *correct* or to pronounce a foreign language like a native because appropriateness in expression is linked to basic attitudes about how people should interact with one another and their social values.

Variation is socially meaningful. Sending messages not only involves sharing information; it also, *at the same time*, involves trying to accomplish one of several social functions. Among these are:

1. *Establishing or maintaining one's social status.* A British person may use phrases such as "to have one's bath" (not "to take a bath") or "false teeth" (not "dentures") to establish that he or she is a member of the upper class. Similarly, an American who never uses colloquial expressions such as "ain't" or "gosh" or uses Latin expressions such as *non sequitur* or *ad hominem* may be working to maintain the impression that he or she is a member of an educated class.

2. *Establishing or maintaining social group membership.* A person may deliberately speak like a jazz musician to indicate membership in a jazz group (jazz musicians have many expressions that they uniquely use). Also, in most countries it is essential for academics to speak and write in a particular way to show that they belong to the academic subculture. A third well-known example is the language of teenagers. If young people don't use the popular expressions of their generation, they are not accepted by their peers.

3. *Showing respect or deference.* In French, use of the pronoun *vous* (formal "you") indicates greater respect than use of *tu* (familiar "you"). In Chinese, people are addressed by their occupational titles to show respect, hence "Manager Wong" or "Engineer Li."

4. *Showing intimacy.* In Russian, use of diminutives indicates intimacy. Thus, friends normally use nicknames with diminutive suffixes, such as *Ninochka* (Nina) or *Boren'ka* (Boris). The greater the intimacy and affection, the greater the proliferation of such diminutive forms. Pronouns are also used to signal intimacy versus distance. In French, use of the pronoun *tu* shows greater intimacy than use of the pronoun *vous*, and the same is true of such languages as Spanish, German, and Russian.

5. *Setting yourself apart from the group.* If you are normally a member of a jazz group but refuse to use their special expressions and phrases, you may be trying to show that you are no longer a member of the group. When American blacks refuse ever to use Black English, choosing instead the English used by middle class whites, they may also be setting themselves apart deliberately from other blacks.

As native speakers, we have little difficulty with referential or social meanings within our own social group because we learn early on how to recognize both meanings intended by a speaker. However, once outside our own social group, we may not be as effective in sending and receiving messages and, as a result, misunderstandings may occur much more frequently. This potential for misunderstanding usually increases many fold once we speak a new language. As language learners we need to be aware that misunderstanding may come from using a form inappropriately or from misinterpreting the intention of an expression. Because the form a message takes is determined so strongly by social meaning, a language learner must be sensitive to how important social messages are sent in order to properly express both referential and social intentions.

THE THREE ACTIVITIES OF COMMUNICATION

There are three basic activities we engage in during the communication process: we express our intentions (send messages), we interpret intentions (receive messages), and we negotiate the intention of the messages that we both send and receive.

Expressing Intentions

You have probably heard someone say, "John *says* one thing and *means* another." As a native speaker, you always need to interpret others' messages and express your own messages in ways that are understood. This is not an easy matter, and people often ask for clarification. People frequently ask, "Did I understand you to mean . . .?" In other words, it is quite common to hear what a person says but not understand his message, either because of the way his sentence was organized or the context in which it occurred. Sometimes, we recognize that others have misunderstood our meaning and we may try to correct their interpretation by saying something like, "What I meant to say was . . . ."

While we are learning our native language, much parental effort is directed toward teaching us to express our intentions in a *socially acceptable* manner and to interpret the intentions of others. This process begins at a very young age and, for some, continues into adulthood. An example is the often heard parental instruction: "If you want a cookie (some milk, your doll), you will have to ask politely."

Because this training is such an integral part of our early language training, we come to expect that there is certainly only one *right* way to send and receive messages. *Right* means that we learn to evaluate others' messages according to our own rules of interpretation and may act very negatively when messages come in forms we don't understand or expect.

Learning to translate our intentions into a new language involves many things. It means, for instance, learning how to show agreement, when and how to hide feelings, how to make a request, how to start a friendship, how to pay a compliment, and how to accept or decline an invitation.

Interpretation

Learning to interpret what others mean is also complex. Because we learn early to interpret meanings by the *form* of expression a person uses, there is much room for misunderstanding. This may lead us to make value judgments and become convinced that a speaker is insincere, dishonest, or disrespectful when we misread the intentions or the significance of a message within a social setting.

One example of the need to use and understand socially appropriate messages is in the determination of when a speaker has said no. In many languages and societies, people don't usually say no **Don't jump to** directly. Instead, they have less direct ways of ex- **conclusions.** pressing refusal. The foreign speaker needs to recognize the ways in which this is done. For example, in Hispanic culture it is considered inappropriate for servants to say no directly to their employers. Instead, the social norm requires the servant to reply to a request from an employer with the form *mañana*. Although a literal translation of *mañana* is "tomorrow," the most frequently intended meaning for it in this situation is simply "no." But, this is a polite no, since the request has not been refused directly, just postponed. A non-native employer will wait a long time for service if he or she relies on the literal meaning of the word *mañana*.

Still another example of misinterpretation relates to who may initiate a conversation. In some Asian languages, such as Chinese, Japanese, or Korean, children do not usually initiate conversations with adults and do not speak unless spoken to. In contrast, American children are free, and even encouraged, to initiate conversations with adults. Similarly, whenever there is a perceived difference in status—for example, between student and teacher—the inferior usually does not initiate verbal contact. So, if you are a teacher, Asian students will not talk to you unless you talk to them first. This, incidentally, can create the mistaken impression that Asians are passive or that they do not understand what is going on.

As foreign language learners, we need to be on the lookout for the appropriate way to express ourselves. When native speakers get angry, look confused, or laugh at our speech, it's probably because our way of expressing ourselves is inappropriate rather than grammatically incorrect. We also need to be aware of our own possible misinterpretations of others. If we find ourselves confused or angry, we need to back up and seek the source of the problem in the flow of conversation and the style of our expression. This process of interpretation and reinterpretation should not discourage us, since even in our native language, we continue to improve our means of expression and techniques of understanding others throughout life.

Negotiation

A speaker's meaning is not always perfectly clear, and, in some cases, a message might be deliberately ambiguous. Hence, you will note that native speakers often negotiate meaning by (1) asking whether a particular story was meant to be a joke, (2) asking whether a statement was intended as a compliment or as an insult, or (3) saying that they don't understand a speaker's intention and need clarification. Negotiation is an important part of any communicative exchange. When speaking a foreign language, we need to discover when a statement is negotiable and how to indicate that a statement we have made is negotiable.

Negotiation is possible and, indeed, often expected in the case of invitations and in saying *no*. In American English, an invitation is sometimes issued in such a way that it cannot be negotiated—that is, the date and time are fixed. On other occasions, some seemingly non-invitations can be negotiated. When someone says, "Let's get together soon," he or she is usually *not* issuing an invitation. However, if the sequence continues and the other person says something like, "I'd love to. Would you like to set up a time now?", the second party would have negotiated the situation into an invitation.

Negotiation may also take place to determine whether a response is a definitive no. Recognizing when the word *no* is actually meant takes a great deal of social knowledge and learning. Children often have trouble with this, provoking their parents to express their nonnegotiable intention by saying something like, "I said no and that's *final*."

In conclusion, expressing, interpreting, and negotiating meaning are all parts of the normal communication process. As foreign-language learners we need to check that our messages are interpreted appropriately. We can do this by watching our listener's facial expressions and noting whether the next comment is an appropriate reply to our intended message. Equally, we can monitor ourselves for misunderstanding by checking our own emotional responses.

Finally, we should note that monitoring a written message is much more difficult. Since we do not have the same sort of immediate feedback, we must be even more careful that we express ourselves in an appropriate mannner and that we have understood the writer's intentions.

PROBLEMS IN SENDING AND RECEIVING MESSAGES

Many things get in the way of expressing and interpreting messages. In this section, we will focus on two major causes of mis-

Note regional variation. interpretation: regional and social variations of expression. In the next section, we will focus on the importance of nonverbal behavior: body language, facial expressions, gestures, silence, and the like.

First of all, it's important to bear in mind that language varies from city to city and region to region. Such differences may cause a language learner some difficulty both in understanding speakers from other areas and in being understood. Sometimes inappropriate use of regional speech can lead to humor or, worse, anger. For example, although the word *papaya* is used in most of Latin America, it is considered obscene in Cuba, where the fruit is instead called *fruta bomba*. Use of the label *papaya* in Cuba may evoke a punch in the nose, though a clearly identifiable foreigner may get away with just a laugh.

Secondly, students need to pay attention to variations based on social differences, since misuse of these may be amusing or insulting. Equally, hearers may miss important messages if they are unaware of the social message inherent in a turn of speech. Some examples of social variation are the following.

Variation according to sex, social status, social role, or age. In Japanese, the sentence final particle *ne* typically indicates that the speaker is female. American women tend to use "reduplicated" adjective forms (such as itsy-bitsy or teeny-weeny) more frequently than men. Russian women use more diminutive nicknames.

Professionals typically use technical language to heighten acceptance of their authority: unless they are trying to be folksy, doctors never say *tummy* or *belly*; instead they use the more technical word *abdomen*. People often use baby talk when speaking to children or to sweethearts. In Eastern American English, speakers of higher social status are usually called *Mr.* plus last name, while lower-status persons are called by first name or last name only. In Jamaican English, the meaning of the term *supper* varies greatly according to the speaker's social class. Among the upper-middle class, *supper* is a light meal eaten between 10:30 P.M. and midnight. Among the lower-middle class, the term indicates a medium-size meal eaten between 4 and 6 P.M.. However, among peasants, it is a light meal eaten between 7 and 8:30 P.M.

Variation according to relative social difference. In many societies, it is essential that participants in a conversation adjust their language
Show respect. to reflect their relative social status. In Japanese and Javanese, it is impossible to speak to someone without indicating a judgment of relative status. Thus, when Japanese meet for the first time, they exchange calling cards that give strong clues to social status. During an initial bow, the participants glance at the cards, assess the relative status of their conversational partners, and decide on the appropriate speaking level. Similarly, Javanese adjust their speech to a variety of social variables, including the relative status of the hearer. To illustrate how much variation there can be, here are two versions of the Javanese question, "Are you going to eat rice and cassava now?"

High form: "Menapa spandjenengan baḍe ḍahar   sekul kalijan
Low form: "apa   kowé   arep mangan sega lan

             kaspé samenika?"
             kaspé saiki?"

Variation according to social situation and setting. We often adjust our language to fit the occasion. For example, when giving a speech or socializing with strangers, we tend to use more formal language than when we are sitting and drinking with friends. We try to avoid swear words and use words like *powder room* rather than *toilet* or *john*. We greet a group of friends with *Hi, fellows!, Hi there!,* or *Greetings!* On the other hand, we open an address to a distinguished gathering with *Ladies and Gentlemen.*

Nonverbal Communication

Many misunderstandings in cross-cultural communication are due not only to language problems but also to ignorance of nonverbal

The body speaks too. cues. Learning a language is only the first step in beginning to communicate with persons from different cultures. In all societies, how you move your body or the expressions on your face are usually an important part of any message. Here are some movements that may communicate as much or more information than words.

Eye contact. In some societies, among them the United States, one shows respect for conversational partners by looking them in the eye from time to time. Not to do so may be interpreted as a sign of disrespect, disinterest, or even untrustworthiness. In many Asian societies, however, looking someone in the eye, especially a superior, is considered very disrespectful. A junior person must always keep eyes cast downward when speaking to elders or superiors.

Smiling. The timing of a smile also carries a message. Rules for when to smile vary greatly from society to society. Americans smile at strangers to signal friendliness and politeness. In much of Asia, however, smiles are reserved for friends and intimates, and smiling at strangers signifies sexual invitation, intrusiveness, or simple-mindedness. Hence, Americans may appear superficial or impolite to Asians, who, in turn, seem hostile, sullen, and unfriendly to Americans. In some societies, it is important to cover your mouth when smiling or laughing.

Kissing. Russian men find it quite normal to kiss each other under emotional circumstances. For instance, Russian Prime Minister Brezhnev kissed President Carter on the occasion of their signing an important agreement. In the United States, however, only women are allowed such public display of emotion. Arabs meet visiting dignitaries by hugging them and kissing them on the cheek. A nervous, jittery reaction from a visitor would hurt local sensibilities. In Japan, neither men nor women are allowed to kiss in public—one is supposed to keep one's emotions quite private.

Handing and handling things. In Islamic cultures, the right hand (often called the "sweet one") is used for eating, while the left is used for bathroom functions only. Nothing is more insulting than to be handed an object with the left hand. Asians are taught to use both hands in giving an object to another person or in receiving an object. The casual American way of using either hand is seen as rude.

Pointing. Whereas pointing with the index finger is common in the United States, in Java, Indonesia, it is considered very rude to point with anything but the thumb. In other societies, pointing is done with other parts of the body, such as the lower lip or the head.

Posture. In Asian countries, posture is a strong indicator of respect. One does not cross feet or legs in the presence of a superior. It is also important to remain physically lower than a respected person. Thus, a Thai, upon seeing an older woman, may show his respect by sitting down in the only available chair. Also, in Thailand, showing the bottom of one's feet is very disrespectful. Hence, Americans who put their feet up in front of Thai friends would be considered rude.

Touching. The rules governing how and when to touch another person vary greatly and are emotionally charged. In the United States, it is common for members of the opposite sex to hold hands if they are romantically involved, but members of the same sex never hold hands unless they, too, are romantically involved. In contrast, in Asia, members of the opposite sex *never* touch in public, since this would be considered an immodesty or a sexual innuendo. On the other hand, in much of Asia, Russia, the Middle East, and Latin America, heterosexual male friends can be seen walking arm-in-arm in the streets or holding hands during conversation. In Japan, touching between most adults in public is rare—even a handshake is absent. And in Thailand, petting someone on the head, even a child, is very disrespectful.

Bowing. In Japan, bowing at introductions and on meeting acquaintances is essential to demonstrate proper respect. No real communication can be conducted without the appropriate degree of bowing.

Head-shaking. Most cultures have ways of moving the head to signify *no*, but the techniques differ significantly. Most Europeans signify *no* by moving the head from side to side. In Bulgaria and Turkey, *no* is signified by throwing the head back and returning it to normal position.

Gestures. While people all over the world use gestures to communicate, the number permitted and their interpretation vary widely. The same gesture can mean completely different things in different societies. For example, the American sign for *okay*, with thumb and forefinger together, may mean either *okay* or *zero* in France, but it is considered obscene in Brazil. Hand gestures for *goodbye* and *come here* have exactly opposite interpretations in the United States and Latin America. In some of Asia, only children can be called by using a hand motion.

Spatial distance between speakers. The number of inches or feet between speakers is an important social message whose meaning varies from society to society. For example, Latin Americans usually stand closer to their conversational partners (either male or female) than do North Americans. North Americans only stand close when they wish to say something fairly intimate. Hence, Latin Americans interpret normal North American speaking distance as unfriendly, whereas North Americans see Latin American closeness as pushy and discomforting.

Medium. There are clear cultural rules for whether a message should be typed, written, or printed. Rules also often dictate whether a message should be delivered in person, by phone, or through a third person.

Noise. Noises that are considered good form in one culture are often frowned upon in another. Some Asians sip liquids loudly, smack their lips, and belch to indicate their enjoyment of food. (Exceptions are Japanese women and Filippinos, who try to eat unobtrusively.) Most Americans find this behavior in very poor taste.

Silence. In many societies, silence is the correct response to certain questions or requests. In the United States, if silence is the response to a request, it usually means *no*. In Britain, it is often interpreted as *maybe*. But in Iran, if a woman responds with silence to an offer of a marriage partner it means *yes*. Among some American Indians, long silences are common when social situations are unclear.

In Japanese, it is quite acceptable to leave sentences unfinished or leave some things unsaid. In conversation, a Japanese usually wants to find out more about his partner and, therefore, falls silent in order to do so. Most Westerners interpret such silences as lack of comprehension and will either repeat or elaborate on what they have said. In addition, silence in Japanese may also mean *no* and this, too, may be misinterpreted.

Thus, to communicate effectively, you need to know more than grammar, vocabulary, and how to make sentences. Knowing when *not* to speak may be just as important as knowing *what* to say. You need sensitivity to how intentions are expressed, interpreted, and negotiated; the interplay between referential and social meaning; how language varies according to social and regional boundaries; and the role of nonverbal behavior.

All of this may seem like a lot to keep in mind, and it is. We have presented this information to illustrate that language cannot be approached mechanically and in isolation. Rather, it must be learned as it is used in social settings to accomplish social purposes. While customs may differ from language to language, most social intentions remain the same; everyone seeks to show respect and save face, make requests, give instructions and information, make a point, show intimacy, accept or reject invitations, agree or disagree, take a turn in a conversation, and so forth. Every language learner needs to keep these purposes in mind and find the socially appropriate way to express them.

Finally, it is important to bear in mind that most people make many allowances for error—at least in the beginning—so don't be afraid to try something out while noting the reaction of the hearer. Through trial and error, your conversation and understanding will rapidly improve.

Chapter 5

THE NATURE OF LANGUAGE

Language is perhaps the most creative of all human inventions. Since the primary function of language is to carry meaning, and since the number of meanings that people communicate to each other is infinite, language must be very efficient. This efficiency is accomplished through several features.

LANGUAGE IS CREATIVE

To meet the demands of communicating an infinite number of messages, language manufactures, so to speak, two products: individual words and combinations of words. The com-

Innovation. binations are sentences or parts of sentences that constitute messages. One can make sentences that have never been said or written before: *There is a purple horse on the living room couch smoking an apple.* Regardless of whether you believe in purple horses smoking apples in living rooms, you can easily process the sentence. The point is that words are units that can be used in a great variety of ways to build sentences according to the rules of the language. These rules put limits on creativity by making some products incomprehensible: *Purple there a horse apple the living an smoking is couch room on* is gibberish and cannot be processed, although the words are the same as in the previous example.

The same creativity fabricates new words out of preexisting parts: the *-burger* of *hamburger* can serve as a base for *fishburger* and *chickenburger*; the *-ee* of *employee* serves handily in *draftee* and *escapee*; the *de-* of *deactivate* builds *detoxify* and *defrock*. Note that rules keep creativity in check. *desex* is easy to understand, but *sexde* is nonsense.

Thus, creativity allows language to accommodate new meanings and messages through innovative use of existing elements, but rules limit the nature and number of possibilities. This brings us to the next feature of language—its systematic nature.

LANGUAGE IS SYSTEMATIC

A learner may reach a point when he or she is ready to shout: "One more rule and I quit! Is there no end to these rules and exceptions?"

Checks and balances. It may be hard to believe that languages actually do operate with a finite number of rules. True, it may take a long time to learn them all. But once learned, they are stored in the brain and allow the user to generate an infinite set of messages.

Every person who knows a language possesses an appropriate set of rules that allow him or her to understand and produce sentences and to recognize whether a sentence is grammatical. Not all rules are learned consciously, however. Often we deduce a rule from context, so we know that something sounds right or wrong, but cannot explain why. This is the type of knowledge that native speakers possess about their own language. It is also the type of knowledge that a student often acquires in real-life settings.

Since language is governed by rules, the learner must come to grips with the language as a system. There are rules at all levels. At the level of sounds, for instance, rules allow for certain combinations of sounds, but exclude others. This may differ from language to language. In English *m* cannot be followed by *l* at the beginning of words, so one knows right away that *mlin* is not an English word; at the same time, *b* can be followed by *l*, so *blin* might be an English word.

At the word level, rules govern combinations of parts. For example, in English, the elements *-er* or *-ian* must follow the main part of the word, as in *reader* or *librarian*; but placing them at the beginning of the word results in nonsense like *erread* and *ianlibrar*.

At the level of sentences, rules tell us how words are combined. In English, the word order is usually subject—verb—object, as in *Mary drinks coffee* or *John loves Mary*. If this rule is violated, we get *Coffee drinks Mary*, which is ungrammatical, and *Mary loves John*, which has a different meaning.

By limiting the number of possibilities in which the words can be arranged, grammar also helps us to predict what will follow, even if something was missed. For example, when you hear the sentence *Mary had a little . . .*, you can predict that the missing word is a noun. When you hear the sentence *The plumber ... the faucet*, you can at least guess that the missing word is a verb and may suspect that it could be *fixed* or *repaired*.

LANGUAGE SIMILARITIES AND DIFFERENCES

Languages are alike yet different because the people who speak them are alike in their human capacities yet different in a million ways.

In the very broadest sense, all languages share some common features, yet learners can be surprised and perplexed that a new language does not express things in the same way as their native language. On the other hand, discovering the similarities between a new language and one's native language is always a delight.

Pronunciation

A new language may have the same sounds as your own language, but they may be pronounced in slightly different ways. For in-

Vive la difference!

stance, English, French, and Spanish all have the sounds *p*, *t*, and *k*, but their quality differs. In English, these sounds are pronounced with a slight accompanying puff of air, while in Spanish and French, the air is released gradually.

Grammar

All languages have ways of modifying nouns, but in some, the modifier usually precedes the noun, while in others, the modifier usually follows. For example, in English we say *big house*, but in Spanish we say *casa grande* ("house big").

English, Spanish, and Russian all have words to express existence or presence, but Russian and English have only one verb that means *to be*, while Spanish has two: *ser* and *estar*. At the same time, Russian omits the verb *to be* in the present tense, while English and Spanish do not. As a result:

English	Russian	Spanish
I am a student.	Ya student. ("I student.")	Soy estudiante. ("Am student.")
I am here.	Ya tut. ("I here.")	Estoy aqui. ("Am here.")

Vocabulary

Words in our own language come to us so automatically that we rarely think of their relationship to the reality that they designate. For instance, the English verb *to know* seems so simple and natural to us that we may assume that all languages treat the concept of knowing in the same way. Yet, many languages distinguish between two different kinds of knowing: knowing (recognizing) people and things, and knowing about something—for example, Spanish *conocer* and *saber*, German *kennen* and *wissen*, French *connaître* and *savoir*, Chinese *rènshī* and *zhīdào*.

Another interesting example is the English word *hot*, which refers to the temperature of the air, as in *hot weather;* temperatures of various substances, such as *hot coffee;* and degree of spiciness of foods, such as *hot peppers*. In Russian, a different word for *hot* would be used in each situation, and in Chinese two would be used (temperature vs. spiciness). Thus, both Russians and Chinese would think that the English phrase *hot soup* was very unclear.

Idioms

Some of the most fascinating examples of similarities and differences between languages are found in idioms and special expressions. Language learners are often surprised when a rather unusual expression has a word-for-word equivalent in another language. Just as often, they may be surprised to find that an expression does not have an equivalent in another language or that the equivalent differs in some ways.

Here are some expressions that rather unexpectedly have identical equivalents in English and Russian—two languages which, although related, are quite far apart in most ways: English *to play first fiddle*, Russian *igrat' pervuyu skripku;* English *to shed crocodile tears*, Russian *lit' krokodilovy slyozy;* English *to look for a needle in a haystack*, Russian *iskat' igolku v stoge sena*.

Here are some expressions that have the same basic meaning but cannot be translated literally: English *to hit the ceiling*, Spanish *tomar el cielo con las manos* ("to take the sky in one's hands"); English *to know something inside out*, Russian *znat' vdol' i poperyok* ("to know something lengthwise and crosswise"); English *to have nine lives*, Spanish *tener siete vidas* ("to have seven lives"); Russian *dvuzhil'nyi* ("one with two lives"); English *when in Rome do as the Romans do*, Russian *v Tulu so svoim samovarom ne ezdyat* ("don't go to Tula [a city famous for its samovars] with your own samovar").

On the other hand, there are no equivalents in English for the Spanish *cara de viernes* ("Friday face," or a "thin, wan face"); *decir cuatro verdades* ("to tell four truths," or "to speak one's mind freely"); *saber más que las culebras* ("to know more than the snakes," or "to be cunning"). At the same time, no language seems to have an equivalent for the English expression *to go bananas.*

It is important that you have some notion of the nature of language since that knowledge will help you in your language mastery. Knowing that the number of rules of a language are finite will make this task less imposing. Using what you know about language will mean that there is less to learn. Recognizing that language is creative should help you approach the task as a challenge which is open-ended rather than defined by a narrow vista. Learning a language is a complex but well-defined task; defined by the rules of a language and by the similarities which languages may share.

Part 2

HOW TO BE A BETTER LANGUAGE LEARNER: LEARNING STRATEGIES

FIND YOUR OWN WAY

It is important to remember that unless you can take charge of your own learning you will probably not succeed. You know yourself **Take charge.** best and should, therefore, use your self-knowledge to guide your studies regardless of your teacher's methods or what the textbook tells you to do.

As mentioned earlier, people learn in different ways. Some need to be very analytical: they need a rule for everything. Others are more intuitive: they gather examples and imitate. Some need lots of repetition; others require less. In a classroom situation, the teacher cannot tailor the approach to each individual student. Therefore, you cannot rely entirely on your teacher to tell you how to study. You yourself need to experiment to discover what works best for you. Following are some suggestions.

Pay attention to your own learning successes. Take, for instance, vo- **Experiment for yourself.** cabulary learning. A memory technique that helps one person may not help another. Here are some options to try.

1. Put the foreign language words in one column and their translations in another. Study the list from beginning to end; then study it backwards.

2. Put the words and their definitions on individual cards or slips of paper; then study them in varying order.

3. Study the words and their definitions in isolation; then study them in the context of sentences.

4. Say the words aloud as you study them.

5. Write the words over and over again.

6. Tape record the words and their definitions; then listen to the tapes several times.

7. Underline with a colored pencil the words that cause you the most trouble so you can give them extra attention.

8. Group words by subject matter—for example, fruits, vegetables, professions—and study them together.

9. Associate words with pictures or with similar-sounding words in your native language.

10. Associate words with situations—for example, medicines with illnesses.

There are also a number of techniques for studying pronunciation. See which of the following work for you.

1. Listen carefully and repeat aloud after your teacher or a native speaker on tape or in real life.

2. Repeat silently to yourself.

3. Tape record yourself and compare your own pronunciation with that of a native model.

4. Ask native speakers to listen to your pronunciation and comment on your strengths and weaknesses.

5. Ask native speakers how a specific sound is formed and watch when they speak. Then go home and practice in front of a mirror.

6. Practice a sound separately at first; then use it progressively in words, sentences, and, eventually, tongue-twisters.

7. Make a list of words that give you pronunciation trouble and practice them.

8. Listen to native speakers of the foreign language when they speak *your* language and note their pronunciation mistakes.

9. Pretend that you are a native speaker of the language you are studying. For example, pretend you are a Spaniard, Italian, or Japanese speaking English. Sometimes this technique helps people relax.

As for grammar, note whether you retain a rule better when you do specially designed exercises (for instance, filling in blanks or changing word forms) *or* when you are required to communicate a message in speaking or writing. Determine which exercises seem to help you most: translations, mechanical drills, answering questions, compositions, and so forth. Also note whether you find written or oral exercises more helpful and whether you retain a rule

better when it is given to you before practice or when you deduce
your own rule.

Learn from others. *Pay attention to the learning successes of others.* Ask other students how they got the right answers and how they successfully memorized something, and see if their strategies work for you too. For example, if someone guesses a word that you did not recognize, ask how he or she did it. Sometimes it is helpful to look at how others organize their notes, rules, and vocabulary lists. You can also ask other students how they organize their practice, where and how they seek out native speakers to talk to, and the like.

Eye or Ear? *Use both your eyes and your ears.* Experiment to see if some tasks are better accomplished through the *eye*, while others are better accomplished through the *ear*. For example, you may find that listening to tapes helps you to improve your oral comprehension and to memorize dialogues; but you may retain vocabulary better if you use flash cards. Remember that applying the same strategy to all tasks does not always work. Try to find strategies that will help you to compensate for your weaknesses.

Continue using the strategies that work for you. Once you have identified the strategies that work best for you, continue to use them, and discard strategies that are ineffective. Don't be afraid to use strategies that work for you even if your teacher says not to.

Be your own master. *Be independent.* Follow the goals you have set for yourself even if they differ from those of your teacher or textbook. For instance, if your goal is to develop speaking proficiency, you can work independently on your pronunciation even if your teacher does not stress it in class.

ORGANIZE

Organization takes two forms in language learning: organizing information about the language and organizing your program of study.

ORGANIZE INFORMATION ABOUT THE LANGUAGE

Learning a new language involves remembering many rules about pronunciation, vocabulary, and grammar. Although your textbook and your teacher will organize this information in certain ways, you will still need to systematize the material for reference and review. The trick is to come to grips with the language as a system and then to devise ways of representing this system for yourself. Below are some hints on how language material can be systematized beyond the textbook.

1. *Organize the study of pronunciation.* Devote a section of your notebook or a separate notebook to pronunciation rules, particularly those that trouble you. For example, if trilled *r's* give you trouble in Spanish, write out words that contain this sound—*radio, perro, barrio,* etc.—and practice them regularly. Ask a native speaker to record these words for you so you can listen and imitate.

2. *Organize the study of vocabulary.* In dictionaries, words are organized in alphabetical order. This is not the best way to organize words for your own use. A better way is to group them according to some principle. For instance, you can group words by generic categories: furniture, money, foods, verbs of motion, and so forth. Or you can organize them according to the situations in which they occur: under *restaurant,* you can put *waiter, table, menu, eat, bill.* Or you can organize words by function: greeting, parting, thanks, conversation openers, etc. Or, instead of making a running list, you can put each word on a separate card so you can reorganize them in different ways, for example, color coding for parts of speech.

There are also several kinds of flash cards that are available commercially. On each flash card, write a sentence that illustrates how the word may be used, particularly if it is a verb. If you are studying Chinese, character flash cards are a must.

3. *Organize the study of grammar.* Construct your own grammar tables in the way that makes the best sense to you. When reviewing these tables, add any new information you may have acquired. For instance, you can make a table of verb conjugations in different tenses, noun declensions, prepositions with the cases they require, etc. Each time you learn a new word belonging to a particular category you have set up, enter it in your table. This is especially important if the word is an exception to a rule and needs special attention. Note also that there are various kinds of commercially available study aids for grammar, such as verb wheels.

ORGANIZE YOUR OWN PROGRAM OF STUDY

Effective study habits are one of the key ingredients of language mastery. You need to organize your study habits and follow through on your plans. Here are a few suggestions.

1. *Establish a regular schedule.* Language is learned in small bits, so try to establish a regular schedule for studying and stick to it. You achieve little by cramming only from time to time. After all, you didn't learn your native language all at once. In fact, it took you quite a while to master all its intricacies, so give yourself the same chance when learning a new language. Learning must be continuous. Do some studying every day, even on weekends and when there is no homework assignment. Do your exercises as assigned rather than all together at the last possible minute. They do little good if they don't have time to sink in. Finally, find the best time of day to do your studying. Don't do it when you have many other things on your mind or are exhausted. Your mind has to be receptive for learning to take place.

2. *Learn something new every day.* Set up a schedule for learning something new every day in addition to your classroom assignments. This is particularly true of vocabulary: you need to build your vocabulary on your own. A good idea, therefore, is to learn several new words every day besides those included in your les-

sons. Try color words one day, vegetables the next, occupations the third day, and so forth. Pretty soon you will impress everyone, including yourself, with the size of your vocabulary.

BE CREATIVE

In order to master another language, you need to be personally involved. You need to play with the language to develop a feeling

Develop a feel for the language

for how it works. The language must, in some sense, become a part of you rather than remain an external mechanical system that you can manipulate according to a set of instructions. Learning a language is a

little like learning to ride a bicycle. One can describe rather precisely what is involved in bicycle riding, but until a learner actually gets on the bike and takes a few spills, no meaningful learning takes place.

Although it's impossible to draw up a precise list of all possible ways to experiment with a new language, the suggestions below should help to get you started.

1. *Experiment with grammar rules.* Often when people are given a rule, they accept it at face value and do not try to use it creatively. Creativity is necessary, however, because most rules have boundaries that must be discovered in order to use the language effectively. The way to find the boundaries is to keep applying a rule until you discover that it no longer applies. For example, in English, once you know that words ending in -*x* form their plural by adding -*es*, as in *box—boxes*, you can keep applying the rule until you discover that it is correct to say *fox— foxes*, but not *ox—oxes*. By pushing a rule to its limit you develop a feeling for how it works. It becomes *your* rule instead of an *English* rule.

Don't wait for someone to point out a rule; look for it yourself. Sometimes the rules that you formulate for yourself will be more helpful than those given by your textbook or your teacher because they are organized in ways that are clearer to you. In addition, having found them yourself, you may be better able to remember and apply them.

2. *Experiment with new ways of using words.* For instance, if you have learned a verb in one situation, try to use it in another. If you have learned that in Chinese one uses the verb *kāi* ("to open") with respect to lights, try to use the same verb with other appliances. Or, if you have learned the English word *finish* in the context of *to finish work*, try it in a new context, such as *to finish school*. Watch for a listener's reaction to the new combination. If the new phrase turns out to be unacceptable, ask why. In any case, don't wait for the teacher to provide you with all the contexts for a word; experiment with it yourself.

3. *Experiment with recurring parts.* In most languages, there are certain elements that are used for building words in fairly regular ways. If you notice how these elements are combined, it will help you to build your vocabulary. For instance, in English the element -*er* is often used to describe participants in different occupations or activities, as in *reader* and *rider*. In Russian, you have *chitat'*, "to read," and *chitatel'*, "reader." If *pisat'* means "to write," how might Russians say *writer*? In Kanuri, a language spoken in Nigeria, we can note the following pattern:

gana	small	nəmgana	smallness
kura	big	nəmkura	bigness
kuguru	long	nəmkuguru	length

Based on this information, how would one say *good* in Kanuri if *goodness* is *nəmnəla*?

4. *Experiment with language as art.* You do not have to be very advanced in a foreign language to write a short poem. In fact, you may enjoy the experience and learn something about the way the language rhymes. Try writing plays based on the dialogues you have memorized. Some will be very funny through unexpected juxtapositions. Write foreign-language captions for your favorite cartoons. You may discover that humor is handled differently in another language and culture. Create foreign-language captions for a book of photographs or paintings. You may not be a Shakespeare, but you will enjoy your experience and learn from it in many unexpected ways.

5. *Play games.* An often overlooked way to practice another language is to use it in playing games. Some foreign-language games are available commercially, and many others do not require special equipment. *Scrabble* sets in several European languages are now commercially available. Here are some other kinds of games you can play in a foreign language: *Show and Tell, Tic-Tac-Toe, Twenty Questions, What's My Line?, Password, Concentration, Simon Says, Hangman, Celebrity Talk Show, Story Circle, Detectives*, riddles, charades, word mazes, word searches, and crosswords.

MAKE YOUR OWN OPPORTUNITIES

Language learning must be an active process. Students who make a conscious effort to practice their foreign language, who seek out op-

Don't just sit there.

portunities to use what they have learned, are more successful than students who assume a passive attitude and rely on the teacher to do the whole job. It is necessary to overcome inhibitions and get into situations where you must speak, read, write, and listen to the foreign language. There is no doubt that exposure to the language in any form leads to increased skill. Below are a few tips on how this can be done.

1. *Perform every classroom activity.* Do every task, even if the teacher does not call on you. For example, if the teacher asks someone else a question, make up your own answer too. Complete exercises in your head when it is someone else's turn, and check your answers against theirs. Listen to the other students and to the teacher as he or she corrects them.

2. *Ask questions in the foreign language.* By asking questions, you invite people to speak directly to you, which provides extra practice. Always try to ask the native speakers in their own language because it predisposes them to answer in their own language as well. As soon as you start studying a foreign language, you should learn how to ask such things as: "How do you say that in . . . ?", "Can I say . . . ?", "Is it correct to say . . . ?", "What is the word for . . . ?" Such simple questions offer countless opportunities for learning.

3. *Interact with native and skilled speakers, including your teacher.* Feel free to speak with your teacher outside of class. Together, you can use your new language to discuss a wide variety of topics. Also

61

try to find native speakers on your campus or in your neighbor-
hood. Many colleges have international student programs or clubs
that you can join. Many cities have ethnic neighborhoods with
stores, restaurants, movies, and sometimes even a newspaper or
radio or TV program. Visits to such neighborhoods will give you an
opportunity to try out dialogues you have memorized in class. Unlike your fellow students, a native speaker in a store or restaurant
will not know the other half of the dialogue and will give you
unexpected responses—and this is exactly when learning will take
place.

4. *Interact with classmates or other students in your language program.* Talking with your classmates or other students taking the
same language can be an easy and enjoyable way to get some practice. You may also find that you feel less inhibited about trying out
new things. Many language departments have language clubs.
These usually provide an opportunity to meet other students, grad-
uate teaching assistants, and faculty with whom you can practice
your newly acquired language. They also offer cultural activities,
such as foreign-language movies, music, songs, and informal meetings with interesting people. In addition there are excursions,
dances, cooking classes, summer camps, and many other programs
that can add to your knowledge of the language and its culture.

If you are living in a country where the language is spoken, put
yourself into situations where you will have to communicate. Make
phone calls, go shopping, run errands, ask people for directions or
help, and so forth. You may have to make an effort to overcome
your initial inhibitions.

Best of all, make friends with people who speak the language
you are studying. A sustained relationship provides the motivation
to communicate and takes away the anxiety involved in speaking to
strangers. Friends will also know your language level and will try to
tailor their speech to your ability.

5. *Listen to the language regularly.* It is important that you listen to
the language on a regular basis. Listening to the language will not
only sharpen your comprehension skills, but will also allow you to
practice pronunciation and speaking. Depending on how advanced
you are, you may select different kinds of listening materials.

If you are a beginner, you will benefit from listening to tapes,
based on the materials you use in class. It is usually easier to memorize dialogues when you practice them with a recording. Repeating after the speaker on the tape will improve your pronunciation

and fluency. Later, when you are more advanced, listening to taped lectures, stories, and interviews is a good way to improve your comprehension and learn additional vocabulary and grammar. In addition to language tapes especially prepared for your course, try to listen to foreign-language radio broadcasts (a short-wave receiver is required for the Voice of America, which broadcasts in dozens of different languages), watch foreign-language TV, and attend foreign-language movies.

Listening to records of foreign-language songs is also both enjoyable and profitable. Many learners find a song easier to remember than a dialogue. Songs have emotional and artistic appeal that many contrived dialogues do not. In addition, the tune helps in recalling the words.

The first time that you listen to any taped passage in your foreign language, you may not understand a great deal. At first, try only to get the gist of it; then listen again and again. You will find that you will understand more each time. Above all, remember that you need not understand every word you hear.

6. *Read something in the foreign language regularly.* When choosing reading material, look for things that you can understand without relying too much on a dictionary. A page a day is a good way to start. As you advance, you will find that you can increase both the quantity of pages you read and their level of difficulty. To motivate yourself, choose subjects that interest you. Seek out newspapers and magazines as well as books. Find a magazine, for instance, that reflects your personal interests, whether politics, sports, or art. If you enjoy food, buy yourself a cookbook in the language you are studying. Take out a subscription to a foreign-language newspaper or magazine. Many people find that illustrated foreign-language magazines are easier to read because the pictures provide many clues.

7. *Write in the foreign language regularly.* Writing is a good way to practice what you already know while learning how to compose themes in a foreign language. Find your own reason for writing if your teacher does not assign compositions on a regular basis. A pen pal is good motivation. You will learn a lot by trying to communicate with someone who shares your interests but comes from another culture.

Other ways to maintain a regular writing schedule include keeping a diary, writing a story in installments, or summarizing the daily news. If possible, ask a native speaker to comment on your writing to suggest better and more correct ways of expressing your thoughts.

8. *Rehearse silently in the foreign language.* The easiest way to practice is to rehearse silently, since it does not require any particular time, place, equipment, or partner. For instance, you can look at objects and try to name them in your foreign language, or look at persons and try to describe them in detail. For instance you might think: "This is an apple. It is red and shiny. I wish I could eat it. Too bad it is not mine. I wonder if that fellow will let me have his apple. How do I ask him for an apple? What will he answer?"

You can also rehearse everyday situations. For example, after you have conducted a transaction with a salesperson, clerk, or waiter in your own language, pretend that you have to do it in your foreign language. What would the same conversation have sounded like in France, Italy, or Japan? "Two croissants, please. And a cup of black coffee." "Spaghetti with marinara sauce and a bottle of Chianti, please." "Two bowls of saimin and don't forget to bring the chopsticks." Then, when you actually need to say these things in a real-life setting, you will be ready.

People who regularly practice silently often find that it becomes a habit. Interestingly, children learning their first language frequently practice with imaginary partners, have conversations with no one in particular, and talk to objects and toys. They endlessly repeat words and sentences and make up nonsense words and phrases. Apparently these activities are an integral part of language learning for children. There is no reason why they should not also help adults.

LEARN TO LIVE WITH UNCERTAINTY

Learners of a new language often find themselves in ambiguous situations. Ambiguous situations are characterized by complexity, novelty, unexpectedness, or lack of clear-cut solutions. They arise when a person does not understand a sentence, paragraph, or conversation because it contains unfamiliar words or structures. Persons who dislike uncertainty tend to become confused, withdraw from the situation, give up, or avoid further contact with the language. They prefer safe situations in which everything has been rehearsed, drilled, and explained. Such behavior is not constructive because language students must learn to cope with uncertainty. Here are a few suggestions that may prove helpful.

1. *Avoid heavy reliance on a dictionary.* Instead, begin by reading a page and lightly underlining in pencil all the items you do not understand. Then read the page again. The second reading will clear up some of the confusion. Erase the lines under items that you now understand. Repeat the process two or more times, reading through the entire page. After the last reading, look up only those items that really prevent you from getting the gist of what you have read. After doing this for a while, you will find that you do not really need to understand every word in order to glean the basic information. In fact, a bit of uncertainty is not harmful. It happens even in your own language every time you read new information, but you usually continue reading in the hope that things will become clearer. And they usually do. The same happens in a foreign language.

2. *Don't get flustered.* People can really get frustrated when they don't understand what another person is saying to them. Some common reactions are: What did he say? What should I say? I feel stupid! Such responses are, of course, nonproductive.

The easiest solution to such an uncomfortable situation is to play dumb. Lapse into your native language immediately, and tell the other person you did not understand what he said. He will usually respond by translating into your language. The payoff— reduction of anxiety. But what will you have learned? Probably nothing. The conversation will be switched to your language, and you will have missed an opportunity to learn.

Another solution is to take charge of the situation. Using the foreign language, tell the other person that you did not understand and ask him or her to repeat. Your use of the foreign language will show that you wish to continue using it. The person will probably repeat or paraphrase the message and continue the conversation.

Still another, and probably the best, solution is to avoid imply- ing that you did not understand *the whole message* when, in fact, you only failed to understand one or two words. Isolate the words or phrases you didn't comprehend and ask what they mean. This is a very natural approach since we do it all the time in our native language. If you handle such clarifications quickly, the conversation will go on.

Actually, it is really not necessary to understand everything that is said. Try to follow the gist of the message and ask for clarifi- cation at the end, if anything remains unclear.

3. *Keep talking.* When speaking, you may feel uncertain about your ability to get your message across, but don't let this stop you. Some people won't say anything unless they are sure that they can say it perfectly. This is a mistake, however, for especially in the beginning, you can't expect to say things perfectly. When your goal is to communicate, you should simply concentrate on producing a normal flow of speech and not be overly worried about individual items. A spoken message at the time it is needed, no matter how imperfect, is worth many unspoken messages, no matter how per- fect. It is better to say something promptly rather than say nothing at all or take so long to compose your message that you exhaust your listener's patience and kill interest in further communication.

USE MNEMONICS

Mnemonics are techniques that make memorization easier by organizing individual items into patterns and linking things together.

Everything is linked in your mind.

There are many kinds of mnemonic devices. You should experiment with different ones to see which work best for you. Here are some you may want to try.

1. *Use rhyming.* Items that rhyme are often easier to remember. When memorizing a list of words, see if some rhyme with each other or with other words that you know. For instance, in Russian, *nash* ("our"), *vash* ("your") and *nas* ("us"), *vas* ("you") should be learned together so that if one is named, the other one will instantly come to mind.

2. *Use alliteration.* Items that start with the same letter(s) or sound(s) may be learned together for easier recall. For instance, English question words start with the letters *wh-*, as in *who, which, where*. In Spanish, question words often start with *qu-* in Russian they start with *k-*. Noting such similarities may help you in both memorization and recall. You will need to associate the correct meanings with specific words.

3. *Associate words with the physical world.* Sometimes a word is more easily learned if it can be associated with color, size, sound, smell, feel, or some other physical characteristic. Any mental image you can form for a word can be helpful. For instance, in trying to remember names of vegetables and fruits, you can associate some with being *red* and *round*, others with being *long* and *green*, and so forth.

4. *Associate words with their function.* Sometimes it helps to associate words with their functions. For example, when memorizing words for furniture, you can group them according to which are used for sitting, which for lying, and so on. Think of your favorite chair or couch.

5. *Use natural word associations, such as opposites.* In your own language, some words tend to be naturally associated. For example, given the word *cold* and asked for another word that instantly comes to mind, most people will mention *hot*. Word pairs like *brother-sister, husband-wife, black-white* are automatically associated in similar ways. Therefore, when learning words in a foreign language, try to form pairs so that when one is mentioned, the other instantly comes to mind.

6. *Learn classes of words.* Sometimes it is helpful to learn words by class, such as color words, days of the week, months of the year, and numbers from one to ten. Try to memorize them in several different orders, however.

7. *Learn related words.* Groups of words that share a common core, such as *white, whiten, whitish*, are more easily memorized together than are groups of unrelated words. If you have a list of words to memorize, try to organize them into groups that share a common core, or try to link a new word with previously learned words that have the same core.

8. *Group words by grammatical class.* Sometimes it helps to organize a list of words by parts of speech: nouns, adjectives, verbs, and so on. Nouns are usually easier to memorize than adjectives and verbs; and adjectives, in turn, are easier to memorize than verbs. You may, therefore, want to spend more time on the more difficult classes of words.

9. *Associate words with context.* You can also associate a new word with the context in which it occurred. Thus, when trying to remember a word, you can think of its context, and the word will come back to you. For instance, in trying to remember the word for breakfast, think of what people usually talk about at breakfast, or think of a conversation about breakfast that you may have had in the recent past.

MAKE ERRORS WORK

Errors are inevitable when you are trying to learn something as complex as a new language. Since most errors result from the learn-

Don't clam up for fear of errors. ing process itself, try to look on them as a potential source of information and a way of improving your skills. Here are a few suggestions on how to deal with errors.

1. *Don't let errors interfere with your participation.* Some people are so worried about making mistakes that they don't say anything unless they are sure they can say it correctly. This leads to a vicious circle: they make errors because they haven't practiced enough, yet at the same time they deprive themselves of the opportunity to practice for fear of making mistakes. Remember that language learning is a gradual process during which the student moves through successive approximations of skill. This process requires much practice, which includes making errors and being corrected. Don't hold back until that magic future moment when you think you will be able to speak without making errors. Without practice, that moment will never come.

2. *Negotiate with your teacher when you want errors corrected.* Sometimes, with all good intentions, a teacher constantly interrupts to correct students while they are trying to say something. When this happens, the students may become intimidated, lose all interest in speaking, and fail to learn to communicate, although they may learn about grammar. At the same time, the teacher may wonder why all the corrections did not improve the students' speaking skills. The answer, of course, is that the students shouldn't be interrupted while they are speaking. Comments should be made later, and only the most serious errors should be corrected. Serious errors are those that cause misunderstanding or that occur repeatedly.

It is a good idea to let your teacher know how you feel about having your mistakes corrected while you are speaking. Ask the

69

teacher to discuss your mistakes after you have finished speaking rather than interrupt your train of thought. If that does not work, change teachers when you can or find native speakers outside of class to practice with. Most native speakers focus on the message rather than the grammatical forms used to deliver it. They will let you know when they don't understand, but will let you speak without interruption.

3. *Learn from your errors whenever possible.* To make errors a source of learning, you must do several things.

- Distinguish, whenever possible, between a casual slip and a recurring error. Casual slips are not serious; even native speakers have occasional slips of the tongue, and you should not worry about them. Errors that you make consistently, however, show that you have not mastered some aspect of the language. They require additional work.

- Try to understand why you consistently make a certain kind of error. Is it because you are not clear about a rule? Or is it that you have totally misunderstood a rule and are applying a nonexistent version of it? Is it because you have not learned the boundaries of the rule—that is, its exceptions? Check your textbook or ask your teacher for clarification.

- Be sure that you understand your teacher's corrections of your work. Ask for additional clarification, if necessary. If you do not study the corrections, both you and your teacher will have wasted your time.

- Incorporate your teacher's corrections into your own system of rules. Your system should constantly expand to accommodate new information.

- When you are doing oral grammar exercises in class, carefully focus on the grammar. At this point, every one of the teacher's corrections should be carefully repeated. Repetition enhances mastery. Many students make it a habit to listen passively to the teacher's corrections with out repeating the correct *form*. This is not a good strategy since by repeating the corrected version you give yourself an opportunity to learn it.

- Note whether additional work has any effect on your performance. Sometimes extra formal practice—such as writing grammar exercises—may not improve your grammar skills. Using the language in real-life situations, however, may be very beneficial. Note whether your strategy for eradicating errors is effective. Amount of time spent may not be as important as type of activity.

4. *Treat spoken errors differently from written errors.* Errors often occur in speech because of pressure to respond quickly. Speaking involves many things simultaneously: choosing meaning, correct grammar, appropriate vocabulary, and proper pronunciation. Since meaning is most important, a speaker often concentrates on it and lets other aspects slip. This is natural, and, as a result, you are likely to make a lot more errors in speaking than in writing. Fortunately, listeners are much more tolerant than readers. Listeners don't have time to analyze every mistake you may make, but readers do. Therefore, when speaking, don't let concern with grammar and vocabulary destroy your fluency. On the other hand, when writing, give extra care to correctness.

5. *Note the relative seriousness of your errors.* As mentioned earlier, some mistakes are mere slips of the tongue and will not happen again. Others tend to repeat themselves. But not all recurring errors are equally serious. While some errors provoke strong reactions from listeners, others do not. Often the mistakes that cause the most reaction are sociolinguistic ones, such as using the informal Spanish *tú* to address your elderly teacher. Grammar errors, such as a wrong ending on a noun or verb, are often overlooked. Even among grammar errors, some are more serious than others. For instance, using the Spanish present tense *voy* ("I'm going") instead of the past tense *fui* ("went") can confuse a listener, while lack of agreement between article and noun, such as *un casa* instead of *una casa* ("a house"), is not very serious because it doesn't affect meaning.

Therefore, note the ways in which listeners react to your errors and concentrate more on those that seem to have left the listener offended, laughing, or confused.

6. *Determine how much error is tolerated in a particular language.* Speakers of some languages are less tolerant of errors made by foreigners than are speakers of other languages. Commonly compared extremes are French speakers, who are very intolerant of foreigners' mistakes, and Chinese speakers, who are very permissive.

Try to gauge the amount of error that is tolerated by native speakers of the language you are studying because it can indicate how much attention you should give to quickly developing correct speaking skills.

USE YOUR LINGUISTIC KNOWLEDGE

As described in Chapter 3, languages often show similarities in pronunciation, grammar, vocabulary, and idioms. In such cases,

Your mind is not blank. you can readily apply what you already know about your own language or other languages you have studied. Such transfer can involve both specific items such as words and expressions, and rules of grammar or word building. Successful language learners rely on what they already know and do not approach a new language as if they knew nothing about it at all. Here are some instances when such an approach will make learning another language easier for you.

1. *Use what you know about pronunciation rules.* If you have studied a language like German, in which final consonants are "devoiced"—that is, *Hund* ("dog") is pronounced with a final *t* instead of a *d*—you can apply the same rule to some other languages, such as Russian, in which the *d* in *rad* ("glad") is also pronounced with a *t* sound. Or, if you have learned how to trill an *r* in Spanish, you can use this skill in Italian, any Slavic language, and even Japanese. But watch out for variations. For instance, the trill may be longer or shorter in some languages.

2. *Use what you know about grammar rules.* If you have studied languages in which nouns have gender, as in Spanish *la casa* ("the house")—feminine; *el libro* ("the book")—masculine, you won't be surprised to find that other languages do the same, although the gender of specific nouns may not coincide. For instance, in French, one has *la maison* ("the house")—feminine; *le livre* ("the book")—masculine, but in German there is *das Haus* ("the house")—neuter; *das Buch* ("the book")—neuter. Rules that apply to verb tenses, word order, and many other grammatical features may be readily transferred from one language to another.

3. *Use what you know about vocabulary.* Many languages are related and contain many of the same words, although they may be pronounced or spelled slightly differently. Words in different languages that come from a common source are called *cognates.* For instance, English *mother,* Spanish *madre,* and German *Mutter* look similar because they all originated from the same parent word. Languages also borrow words from each other, either with or without adjustments to make them conform to grammar rules, as in the Russian verb *parkovat'* ("to park"). Similarities in vocabulary should be noted because they simplify your learning task.

However, beware of differences. Words that look the same but differ in meaning can cause problems. For example, *asistir* in Spanish does not mean "to assist"; it means "to attend." In Russian, *magazin* means "store," not "magazine," and *intelligentnyi* means "educated" not "intelligent."

Sometimes the differences are more subtle, so you have to consider the context in which the similar word is used. For instance, in English the word *class* means both a *lesson* and a *room*: *I just had an English class,* and *This class is very hot.* In Russian *klass* can only be used in the second sense.

If a language you have already studied has two words that have only one equivalent in your own language, be on the lookout when you study new languages. For example, if you know that the verb *to ask* has two equivalents in Spanish (*preguntar,* "to ask a question," and *pedir,* "to ask for something"), you should not be surprised that there are two equivalents in Russian (*sprashivat'* and *prosit'*), in French (*demander* and *prier*), and in Chinese (*wèn* and *qǐng*).

Thus you can see that experience with one language can help you learn another because languages have many similarities. However, although many things can be transferred from one language to another, great caution is required, particularly when it comes to idioms and special expressions. Whenever you encounter a new idiom, check its meaning in a dictionary or ask a native speaker for an equivalent, but avoid literal translation.

LET CONTEXT HELP YOU

The meaning of a word or phrase is clarified by its use in a specific sentence or social situation. The only real way to understand a speaker's message or intention is to guess the meaning, something we all do routinely in our native languages. By guessing and taking risks, you will be able to confirm your understanding of a conversation. You will then learn to note relationships between words, phrases, and sentences in a conversation or text and among the participants in a discussion and grow to understand them better. In order to identify these important relationships, you should use what you know about your own or other languages and about human relationships in general. Here are some contexts that require attention.

Not all words mix.

1. *Pay attention to relationships between individual words.* Be on the lookout for words that are used in contexts not found in your own language. For example, in English, the word *handsome* can describe both living and inanimate objects, as in *handsome young man* and *handsome desk*. In other languages, such as Spanish, different words are used to describe the appearance of people and things. Another example is that in English, you can *shoot* both *tigers* and *baskets*, but in Russian and Spanish, you can only *shoot tigers*, not *baskets*. On the other hand, in Russian, *to open* is used not only with regard to books, doors, and windows, but also with regard to appliances, electricity, and water faucets. In English, people are *tall* and buildings can be either *tall* or *high*, but in Russian and Chinese, there is only one word to describe height. You should be aware constantly of new or different combinations of familiar elements in the speech of your teacher, fellow students, and native speakers. Another way to determine the range of a vocabulary item is to ask questions about it: "Can X (a noun) be *handsome*?" Can Y (another noun) be *handsome*?", and so forth.

2. *Use phrase or sentence context to derive meaning.* In most languages, the meaning of a word can only be derived from the context of a sentence. In English, this is true of such verbs as *to take* and *to do*. Look at the variety of meanings associated with these verbs: *to do over* ("to redecorate"), *to do out of* ("cheat"), *to do in* ("to kill"), *what's doing at the office* ("happening"); or *to take ballet* ("to study"), *the vaccination took* ("was effective"), *to take after* ("to resemble").

3. *Use conversational context to derive meaning.* Often you may not be able to understand a particular sentence when you consider it by itself. You need to know how it relates to other sentences in order to really understand it. For example, in Russian, to ask directions to the subway, you would say: *Vy ne skazhete gde tut metro?* ("Can you tell me where the metro is?") The response—*Ne skazhu* ("I won't tell you")—may strike you as a little annoying or strange. However, a succeeding sentence, such as *Ya ne zdeshniy* ('I'm not local") indicates that the intended meaning of *ne skazhu* is not really "I won't tell you" but rather something like "I don't know," or "I can't tell you." You need the second sentence to determine the meaning of *ne skazhu* and to keep you from misinterpreting it.

4. *Pay attention to social context.* Some words gain their meaning largely from social context. For example, in Russian *sestra* means "sister" in the context of a family, but "nurse" in the context of a hospital. The only way to learn and understand these words is in and with the appropriate social setting.

LEARN TO MAKE INTELLIGENT GUESSES

In language learning, it is important to constantly try to decipher the message and the speaker's intention. To do this, you must ap-

Find the right cue. ply what you know about the world and about communication in general. Here are some ways to make intelligent guesses about a message.

1. *Look for the big picture.* In trying to understand a story, conversation, or passage, it always helps to look for the main topic, mood, or setting. This will help you focus your attention and guess other important information. Ask yourself *where* the story or conversation is taking place. Is it in a store? Then there is probably talk about buying and selling. Does it take place in a restaurant? Then the conversation is probably about food. *Who* is involved in the situation? If it is a doctor and patient, one can assume they are talking about health and medicine. If it is a police officer and a tourist, they may be talking about directions. Use what you know about the world to help you guess.

2. *Focus on the important parts.* A key skill in any learning process is identifying the things that are most important. Look for the main topic or message and don't worry about individual words. In this way, you won't waste your energy, and your learning will move ahead more quickly.

3. *Use probabilities.* Like the parts of a puzzle, the parts of a language are connected, so once you see the overall outline, other things may fall into place. In language, there are certain probabilities of occurrence that will help you understand a sentence. For example, if you hear: "They went to the sports arena to buy some . . . ," there is a good chance that the missing word is *tickets*.

It is important to be aware of such probabilities and to play the odds.

4. *Assume that the here and now is relevant.* Assume that what a person says is directly related to something he or she is experiencing at that very minute. Most conversations relate to the present. People commonly talk about the weather, the social setting, their feelings (which are often obvious from their facial expressions), or some action that is under way. So, it is very easy to establish the topic even if you don't know much of the language. Here's an example. A teacher of the Twi language was instructing students in how to barter and bargain in an African market. In the process, she said, "I bought an X (a Twi word the students had never heard before)." At first, the class was stymied. Then they remembered that they were talking about marketing and began guessing what X might be. They asked the teacher: "Is X a fruit or a vegetable?" "What color is it?" "What size is it?" They were able to identify the meaning of X by assuming that the sentence was directly related to the here and now—that is, to the subject they had just been discussing.

5. *Expect some guesses to be incorrect.* Our assumptions are sometimes mistaken—either our rule is useful or it isn't. Don't be discouraged if your first guess is incorrect. Try another. But try to learn from your mistakes and generate better hypotheses the next time.

LEARN SOME LINES AS WHOLES

In the course of studying a foreign language, we often run across sentences or phrases that can be understood from context but can't

Learn gestalts. be analyzed word for word. The best way to deal with such expressions, which are sometimes called idioms, is to learn and use them as wholes, without worrying a great deal about their mechanics. In fact, in many cases, an analysis or explanation may be neither available nor helpful. Here are some ways to cope with idiomatic expressions.

1. *Store idioms or expressions for future use.* The meaning of an idiom or expression is often clarified by its context. Recalling the context in which you first saw or heard an idiom will help you remember and use it correctly. For example, suppose you hear one Spanish speaker saying to another when meeting, "¿Que tal?" (literally: "What such?") with the other answering, "Bien, ¿y tú?". It should not matter too much what *tal* means in this context. The important thing is the whole utterance, the gestalt. Use it next time you have to greet someone. Another example of a gestalt is the Russian combination "vot kak" (literally: "here now") which means "Is that so?". The English word-for-word equivalent, obviously, is nonsensical. Once you find out its meaning, just treat the whole expression as one item or word. Put it away for future use to express amazement.

When using idioms, be sure to watch for the listener's reactions. If the listener does not understand what you said or looks bewildered, you have probably used the phrase inappropriately. Of course, the only way you will learn to use it is by experimenting with it until you find the limits of its use.

2. *Accept some corrections on faith.* Especially in the case of idioms, you may need to accept corrections from your teacher or native speakers without requiring an explanation. Idiomatic expressions may involve grammar or words that you have not yet learned or that are difficult to explain. Adopt each correction, store it, and analyze it later.

3. *Learn proverbs, folk sayings, and the like.* Every language has many proverbs, sayings, and special expressions that are extremely colorful and graphic, although difficult to analyze word for word. If you adopt them, they will make your speech sound more authentic and proficient. For example, in English we say *so-so*, meaning "not particularly good or well"; in Chinese they say *mămă hŭhŭ* ("horse horse tiger tiger"); in Russian one says *tak sebe* ("so to oneself"); and in French they say *comme çi, comme ça* ("like this, like that"). Such phrases can't be analyzed; they must just be used as prefabricated chunks.

4. *Learn parts of songs, poems, commercials, and the like.* Sometimes parts of songs, poems, ads, and commercials are adopted into everyday language. They stick in the mind so easily that people remember them for years. Such turns of speech are most likely to be picked up in informal settings, particularly in the country where spoken. Like other idioms, they defy analysis and must be accepted as self-contained wholes.

5. *Use expressions from textbook dialogues.* Last but not least, don't forget the dialogues that you have learned in class. They can provide ready-made bits of language for use in real-life situations. A line memorized from a dialogue can pop out very quickly because you do not need to construct it yourself. Of course, you can't rely completely on memorized dialogues, but sometimes they can be useful.

LEARN FORMALIZED ROUTINES

Since the primary purpose of learning another language is communication, it is important to identify and learn the ways that native

Learn handy phrases.

speakers organize conversation and accomplish communication goals. Among these are ways of beginning and ending a conversation, encouraging a speaker to keep talking, apologizing, accepting and refusing an invitation, asking for directions, seeking and offering help, and expressing reactions. In any language, there are always routine ways of accomplishing these tasks. It is desirable to learn some of these routines because they show that you are involved and want to converse. Some examples of formalized routines follow.

1. *Learn some phrases for beginning and ending conversations.* Every language has standard greetings, introductions, courtesies, and leave-takings. In English, we begin a conversation with *Hello!* or *Hi!* and may end with *Take care, See you later, I gotta go now,* or *I'll see you.* In telephone conversations, English speakers have clear rules for beginning and ending. When making a business call, the person calling says, *Hello, I would like to speak to so and so, please.* When told to hold the line, the caller will often say *thank you.* When the conversation is over, the conversational partners usually say *goodbye.* However, in Russian formalized routines are different. A typical business call does not require greetings, thank you's, or leave-takings. Instead, *Pozovite Ivanova k telefonu* ("Ask Ivanov to the phone") is a typical opening for a business call.

2. *Learn expressions that show you are paying attention and following the conversation.* In English, we use such comments as *Yeh, Good, My goodness, Uhuh, Wow, Really?, How strange, How interesting,* to encourage a conversational partner. Inserting such phrases at the right times indicates that we understand and are interested.

We also use words and phrases to show that we haven't understood: *I don't understand, What did you say?, What do you mean?, Can you repeat that phrase?, Can you speak more slowly, please?* Such comments are especially useful in the beginning stages of learning another language. It is important, however, to learn the culturally specific forms or you may be misunderstood. For example, in English, when someone is talking and a listener wants to show that he is paying attention he will often say *I know...I know...I know...*, which signals interest and involvement. The counterpart in Russian is *da...da...da...*, which means "yes...yes...yes...". Saying *I know* in these circumstances in Russian would be annoying because it signals to the speaker to get on with the conversation, not that the listener is involved and interested.

3. *Learn how to express your reactions.* You should learn how to express your impressions and comment on an action. In English, we praise or criticize someone with phrases such as *You look nice, What a good idea!,* or *How awful!*

Also learn how to agree and disagree. In English, we use phrases such as *I agree, really, certainly, You're right,* and *I don't agree.* However, rules for expressing one's reactions govern the use of particular phrases with particular persons in particular settings. For example, it would be inappropriate for subordinates to use the phrase *That was a dumb idea* to their superiors. Instead, they might ask, *What do you think of that idea?*

4. *Learn to involve your conversational partner.* It is common to involve one's conversational partner by using expressions that ask for confirmation of preceding comments. In English, we use such questions as *How did you like that?, What do you think of that?, What's your opinion?, Do you agree?* and *Don't you think so?* Use of these indicates that you are interested in and involved with your conversational partner.

Note, for instance, that Spanish speakers often end their statements with *¿no?* or *¿verdad?*, both of which seek the listener's confirmation. The French use *n'est-ce pas?* ("isn't that so?"), the Russians use *da?* ("yes?") and *tak?* ("so?"), and the Chinese use *duì bú duì* (literally, "correct not correct").

5. *Learn ways of managing a conversation.* Conversation-management techniques include:

- Attention getters: *Hey, Mary!*
- Politeness routines: *Thank you very much, Excuse me.*
- Suggestions: *Let's* . . . .
- Requests: *Come here, Wait a minute.*

Again, you need to learn the patterns that are used in the language you are learning. For example, when you don't understand something, you can say several things in English, including, *Excuse me?* and *Please?* In Russian, these would not signal lack of understanding. Instead, the most common responses are *Chto?* ("What?") and *Chto vy skazali?* ("What did you say?"). Translated into English these may sound somewhat rude, but they are normal and appropriate in Russian.

6. *Learn some routines for refusing and accepting invitations.* To avoid seeming rude, you need to learn culturally acceptable ways of refusing and accepting. For example, in Arabic cultures, refusal is often done by saying *God willing.* By saying this phrase without details, such as time and place, you have refused an invitation. If you say *God willing* and give details, you have accepted. English formulas for accepting include phrases such as *I'd love to, How nice of you to invite me,* and *I'll be there.*

7. *Learn to ask for help.* In seeking directions, try to find a formula that elicits a *yes* or *no* response. Hence, ask *Is this the road to Bombay?* or *Does this bus go to Paris?* If you ask questions such as *How do I get to Bombay?*, you may not understand the complicated response that follows.

8. *Learn to offer help.* Every language has standard ways of offering help. For example, in English, service personnel commonly address customers with the phrase *May I help you?* In Russian, the most common phrase is *Chto vy xotite?*, which translates as "What do you want?" In Chinese, service personnel do not say anything, but wait for customers to state what they want.

Use of these formalized routines will help you maintain a conversation. However, be sure to learn the phrases that are appropriate and culturally acceptable in the language you are studying. As you become more advanced, you will learn how to vary the routines to accomplish your social purposes. But at the beginning, the basics are enough to get you through most situations. The trick is to get communication tasks accomplished with limited language skills.

LEARN PRODUCTION TECHNIQUES

Since ongoing exposure and participation in conversations provide the best opportunities to practice and learn another language, it is

You know a lot.

helpful to acquire some techniques for maintaining conversation. Don't let concern for grammatical accuracy and fear of making mistakes keep you from practicing. Here are some conversation techniques you may find helpful.

1. *Use what you know.* Use whatever you know to get your message across, even though you may suspect that there are better ways of saying it. For instance, say *Please give me this,* even though you would rather say *Could you please pass me the salt.* Or, assume that the word in the other language is borrowed from yours and try saying it in the pronunciation of the foreign language. For example, since Japanese syllables almost always consist of a consonant and a vowel, if you wanted to say *bus* in Japanese, you might try to add a vowel and say "busu." You would almost be right because the Japanese for bus is *basu,* clearly a borrowing. Attempting to say something is better than saying nothing at all. In the process, you may even learn the proper way to say what you had in mind.

2. *Paraphrase.* If you don't know or forget the exact word you want, say it in another way. For example, if you forget how to say *warm,* say *not very hot.* If you forget the word for *hat,* say *thing on top of your head.*

3. *Use synonyms.* If a listener has trouble understanding you, try to clarify your intentions by using synonyms, or words that mean the same thing. For instance, when you use the word *instrument* and a listener doesn't understand your pronunciation, if you say *some-*

thing like a piano, violin, or drum, he will probably catch on. Another way of clarifying a statement is to expand it a bit. Thus, if someone doesn't understand your sentence, *He sang yesterday,* adding a descriptive phrase, like *He sang a song yesterday,* may clarify your intention.

4. *Use cognates.* Historically related languages, such as French, Spanish, and Portuguese, or Russian, Polish, and Serbo-Croatian, share many words with similar meanings but somewhat different forms. For example, *activité* in French is *actividad* in Spanish, and *actividade* in Portuguese. In Russian, the word for "people" is *lyudi,* in Polish it is *ludzie,* and in Serbo-Croatian it is *ljúdi.* It is very helpful to try out cognates to keep a conversation going. Beware, though, because similarities can be misleading. For example, the English word *embarrassed* and the Spanish word *embarasada* may look similar, but they have quite different meanings. *Embarasada* means "pregnant."

5. *Repeat.* If you find that someone doesn't understand you, don't give up. There are several things you can do to help your listener understand. You can speak more slowly. You can write or spell a word or phrase. You can try repeating several times. Don't get discouraged. Be creative and find a way to communicate!

6. *Ask for help.* Very often if you ask your conversational partners for help, they will gladly respond. For example, you can ask *What do you call a person who delivers mail?* In this way you will learn a new word and keep the conversation going.

7. *Use hesitation fillers.* It also helps to learn the sounds, gestures, words, or phrases that let your listener know that you are groping for a word or thought. For example, in English some common pause fillers are *well, let's see,* and *you know.* In Chinese, the word *nē gè* ("that") is repeated several times. Note that native speakers use these expressions all the time. This will help you in two ways. First, your listener will know what you are doing and may even try to help. Second, it makes your conversation seem more natural, since we all tend to pause and think from time to time. Think of how you handle such situations in English. Then find a hesitation filler in your new language that makes you feel comfortable.

8. *Use gestures.* You can use gestures or other physical movements to express your ideas. For example, if your conversational partner doesn't understand the sentence *And then I stood up and applauded,* try showing what you mean. Again, this will help keep the conversation going even though one or two words may not be clear.

9. *Avoid problems.* Another way to maintain a conversation is to avoid problem areas. For example, if there are some words that you have difficulty pronouncing, avoid them by using synonyms. Or, if you are unsure of how to use the subjunctive in Spanish, you may avoid trying to express possibility, doubt, and desire. This may limit what you can say, but at least you won't slow up the conversation. You have to be smart about when and how to use avoidance. When correctness is important, you may want to avoid the troublesome area and substitute something you know better. However, if communication is important, avoidance may actually cause misunderstanding. Also, if you feel that you must always be correct, you may avoid so many situations that you won't make progress.

USE DIFFERENT STYLES OF SPEECH

The way in which you say something is often more important than what you say. For beginning foreign-language students, it is diffi-

Variety is the Spice of Life. cult to learn many forms for the same expression or intention. Hence, it is common for teachers and students to rely on a single expression to convey their meaning in the most neutral fashion possible. In some languages, like English, it is relatively easy to find such neutral expressions and thus avoid suggesting anything about social relations. However, in other languages, like Japanese, variation in form is obligatory, and nothing can be said without making a social comment or identifying the nature of social relationships. Since the relationship between form and meaning is so important, you should pay attention to the following.

1. *Observe differences in forms of address.* Note how the teacher addresses students when praising or reprimanding them. Is there a difference? For instance, in some languages, diminutives or nicknames are used when an exchange is friendly, but full or last names may be used when the tone is angry. Note how the teacher addresses male vs. female and older vs. younger students. In most languages, you address people superior in status differently from those that are equal. Hence, learn how to address your teacher and your fellow students according to their differences in status.

2. *Be aware of variation in general.* In listening and reading, watch for variations according to (a) *who* is speaking—you will find that differences in age, sex, and social status may require different speech habits; (b) *where* the action is taking place—setting may determine level of formality, as in conversation at home vs. a formal lecture; (c) *what* is being discussed—forms of speech may change according to the topic of conversation. For instance, an individual *decides* to do something, but a congress *adopts* a resolution.

3. *Look for different ways to accomplish similar purposes.* When native speakers talk, listen for different ways to ask for something, refuse or accept an invitation, greet a friend, apologize, express approval or disapproval, close a conversation, and so forth. Note sentences that seem to accomplish the same social purposes in different ways. Try to identify the social meaning of these differences. For example, compare the following two requests: *Close the door* and *It's cold in here.* Try to discover the difference in their social meanings, when each is used, and who addresses them to whom.

4. *Pay attention to variations used by your conversational or correspondence partner.* Notice the way your conversational or correspondence partner speaks or writes and try to adapt to it. Try out the phrases your partner uses and see whether they are well received. For example, suppose your partner uses two phrases that you suspect mean the same thing: *He was laid back* and *He was very relaxed.* Analyze when he or she uses each one. Are there differences between the settings in which each is used, or does use vary with the people who are present? It often helps to ask whether the two phrases mean the same thing, when each can be used, and with whom.

5. *Learn some slang, especially if you're young.* If you are young, try to learn some slang from native speakers of the same age so that you can converse with them on their own social level. If you say something very formal like *How do you do?* instead of *Hi* or *Hi guys!*, you may find it difficult to make friends. On the other hand, avoid using slang with older people or in more formal circumstances.

ASSESSING A LANGUAGE COURSE

Suppose that you have located several courses in your area. Their prices are right and they're offered at convenient hours. How do you make a final decision? The best solution is to treat the course like any other major purchase—try it out, if possible, and consult other consumers.

1. Ask friends and acquaintances if they have heard anything about the course.

2. Ask for permission to sit in on the class. During your visit:
   a. See how you like the teacher and her approach.

b. Consider, the classroom pace. Is it too slow or too fast for you?

c. Observe the amount of student participation. A course in which students actively participate is usually more productive than one in which the teacher does all the talking.

d. Examine the textbook. If you want to learn to speak and the textbook emphasizes reading, grammar, and translation, you might be well advised to seek a different course.

3. Ask students in the class for their reactions. Ask about homework, grade requirements, and the like. The more you know about the course ahead of time, the better off you will be.

As you can see, you don't have to be an expert to tell the difference between a good and a bad language course. Knowing what you want and using your common sense will help you make the right choice. Your time and money will be better spent if you do some comparative shopping.

Part 3

AIDS
FOR THE LANGUAGE
LEARNER

LANGUAGE TEACHERS

The beginning stages of language learning usually take place in the classroom and are thus molded by the teacher, who deter-

The teacher can't do everything for you.

mines the textbook and the method and creates the classroom atmosphere. It is important to remember, however, that you should not rely totally on your teacher to determine the course of your learning. Without your active input and participation, even the most outstanding teacher will not be optimally effective. You know yourself best; therefore, you should use self-knowledge to determine how you will learn. It is a good idea to discuss your goals and preferred ways of learning with the teacher.

Your teacher's most important role is to model how native speakers communicate. You should therefore constantly analyze your teacher's speech. Listen for pat phrases and note when and how they are used. Notice how your teacher reacts to what you say. Did he or she understand? Laugh? Why?

Your teacher is also an important source of information about how the language is structured, what words and phrases mean, and when they should be used. Check your understanding of a structure by making up sentences and asking your teacher if they are correct. Ask him or her to explain differences in meaning or usage between two words or sentences. Make sure that you understand the corrections in your homework, compositions, and tests.

Negotiate differences.

Your teacher should also be able to provide advice on how to study a foreign language. See if his or her suggestions work for you. If they don't, try to develop your own study techniques.

The teacher also helps set the pace of your learning. If you have trouble keeping up, try to improve your study skills and seek extra help. If you find the pace too slow, ask your teacher for additional materials to reinforce and extend the basic information. In either case, let your teacher know that the pace is not right for you.

Your teacher is also an important source of motivation. By rewarding your progress, your teacher can encourage you toward greater achievement. If your teacher is not a good source of motivation, try to switch teachers as soon as possible.

Some students are self-conscious and find it difficult to talk in front of their teacher because they fear criticism. Instead, they find it easier to communicate with other students or with native speakers who are not teachers. If you feel that way, make sure that you get additional practice outside of class.

In many instances, a language course is taught by a teacher who is not a native speaker and whose accent is inaccurate. Many excellent language teachers recognize this limitation in themselves and supplement the course with tape recordings of native speakers. In fact, students' pronunciation is not affected by whether or not their teachers are native speakers. The important factor is their ability to mimic and their motivation to improve their pronunciation, given exposure to native speech. Thus, if your teacher is not a native speaker, either listen to tape recordings of native speakers or seek opportunities to practice with native speakers outside of the classroom.

On your own. You can study a foreign language without a teacher too. It can be done quite successfully if you use programmed learning materials, tapes, or records *and* have access to a native speaker or speakers. It is also essential to get periodic evaluations of your progress. If you want to or need to study a foreign language that is not taught in your geographic area, or if you need to go slower or faster than a regularly scheduled class, try to find an individualized or self-instructional program.

LANGUAGE TEXTBOOKS

A foreign or second language textbook is designed to provide basic coursework and explanations about how the language works.

A textbook is not a bible. Different textbooks reflect different approaches to language teaching and learning. As a rule, older textbooks emphasized grammar, reading, and translation. The textbooks of the 1950s and 1960s usually focused on listening and speaking. Many featured dialogues to be memorized and highly repetitive drills. In the 1970s, textbooks became somewhat more eclectic, combining elements of several different approaches. Today, textbooks are generally written with the development of communicative competence in mind. They emphasize the ability to use language in practical situations.

Whatever the textbook, it will not contain everything to be covered in a course; neither will all its explanations strictly coincide with those of the teacher. You should, therefore, be prepared to supplement the textbook with your own notes, your teacher's handouts, and other materials. Choosing a textbook is a highly subjective process that is usually left up to the teacher or a committee. Students rarely have any say in the matter. Hence, it is a good idea to try to make the most of any textbook. Blaming the textbook for your failure to learn the language is a lame excuse. Here are some things you can do to supplement your textbook or use it in the most efficient manner.

1. Note additional examples, explanations, and clarifications that your teacher makes or you discover in the appropriate section of your book.

2. Most textbooks have grammar tables either in the individual lessons or at the end of the book. Review these tables regularly,

adding to or modifying them as your knowledge of the language grows.

3. Many textbooks have a vocabulary list at the end that can be used for review or reference. Some textbooks indicate the page or lesson in which a given word occurs. This allows you to check how the word is used in context. For instance, if it is a verb, you can go back and find out which preposition or case goes with it.

4. The dialogues and stories in the book provide models of how things are said in the foreign language. They also show how certain situations are handled—for example, how to disagree, return a compliment, make a telephone call, and so forth. They also use idiomatic expressions in appropriate contexts. Take note of these things as you prepare your oral or written assignments and borrow from the textbook freely.

5. The information in a textbook is sometimes scattered over several chapters without ever being summarized in one place. When this occurs, you should reorganize the material in your notes to make it easier to refer to and understand.

6. Many language textbooks have very useful appendixes. They may include a glossary that defines all words introduced in the text in alphabetical order; conjugations of irregular verbs; tables that summarize major grammar topics; and a grammar index that lists the page numbers on which specific grammar topics are discussed. Be sure that you know what is included in your book's appendixes and how to use this information.

It is important to realize that your textbook is merely one printed source of information about the foreign language, albeit a very important one. As you gain confidence, go beyond your textbook to other printed matter. Look at newspapers, magazines, and easy-to-read books. Even if you don't like your textbook, you can use it to prepare yourself for supplementary materials that you find more interesting.

DICTIONARIES

Most serious language students find it helpful to buy a dictionary fairly early in their studies because it is an endless source of vocab-

There's a dictionary for everything. ulary enrichment. They usually buy a bilingual dictionary (English-foreign language, foreign language-English), a number of which are available for most commonly taught languages. More advanced students often also buy a monolingual dictionary that gives more details about the language. Other kinds of dictionaries can also be helpful from time to time. Among the more useful are a pronouncing dictionary which lists only pronunciation norms, such as stressed syllables, a dictionary of idiomatic phrases, a dictionary of geographic terms, and a dictionary of abbreviations. In addition, there are specialized dictionaries in such areas as sports, music, art, medicine, law, space, and electronics. These are usually available in good libraries. In some languages, monolingual dictionaries may be important even in the early stages of learning because they provide information about declensions and conjugations, list exceptions, and provide examples of how a word can be used in different contexts.

WHEN TO USE A DICTIONARY

Dictionaries offer information about the spelling, pronunciation, meaning, and alternate forms of words. Whenever you need such information, the dictionary is a good place to start. However, it is important to avoid becoming too dependent on it. Remember that meaning can frequently be gained from context even better than from a dictionary, and often more quickly and surely. And while pronunciation is important, a listener's reaction is often a better clue to when you are too far off target. Of course, when writing you will want to refer to a dictionary as necessary for correct spellings or alternate forms. But especially when reading, don't get bogged down—at least at first—by paying too much attention to every word. Look up the most important items, if you must, but try to guess the rest.

HOW TO USE A DICTIONARY

If you encounter a new word in a written text, you may wish to look it up. Remember that foreign alphabets may have a different order

Don't be a dictionary freak.

than in English, and that languages that have inflections (endings) will have only one basic form in the dictionary: nouns and adjectives will be given in the nominative case, verbs in the infinitive. It may take some practice to learn how to look up words. You may have to develop a number of special techniques, depending on the language you are studying.

When you look up a word in a dictionary, whether monolingual or bilingual, you may find that several equivalents are given. You must then decide which equivalent meets your needs. If you are reading, you can probably pick the right equivalent by examining the sentence or paragraph in which the word occurs. If you are still confused, look up one of the forms to see what other words are associated with it and whether they give you a clue.

If you are writing or giving a talk, choose your words with care. Beware of trying to find *exact* equivalents. In every language, words have a range of meanings that are rarely identical. Although there may be exact equivalents, their usages in context may differ. Study the examples given in the dictionary—they should help you understand appropriate usage.

Limitations

Dictionaries are only limited reference guides. They may serve as starting points in understanding a word or phrase, but you must add other information and observations to use them effectively.

LANGUAGE TAPES AND RECORDINGS

Tapes and recordings provide students with opportunities for additional practice on their own terms. Good tapes especially prepared for a course not only allow students to review what has been covered in class, but frequently contain additional exercises that can help clarify difficult points, improve pronunciation, increase fluency, and enhance comprehension. Tapes can provide individualized practice with as many repetitions as needed. They are endlessly patient, always available, and never critical.

Tapes can be used almost anywhere and anytime. The language laboratory is, of course, a good place for listening. But if your lab's hours are inconvenient, then you can always find another time and place for listening to the tapes. That is why a portable tape recorder and set of cassettes can become as indispensable as a textbook and a dictionary.

When beginning to study a new language, you can use tapes to practice pronunciation. Learning to pronounce new sounds takes much individualized practice, and time isn't always available in class. Tapes are especially helpful when you feel shy or uncomfortable practicing new sounds in front of others. Pronunciation tapes and records are available for many commonly taught languages. Ask your instructor for recommendations. Besides individual sounds, one needs to practice the rhythm and intonation of a new language. Tapes can also be helpful with them.

Listening to taped dialogues or texts can ease the tasks of memorization and learning how new words are pronounced. However, when you work without a tape you do not get feedback about your performance. Consequently, you may not realize that you are mispronouncing certain words or that your intonation is incorrect.

When you can simultaneously see a text and hear it on tape, you can improve both your retention and your pronunciation.

Taped grammar exercises can also provide many hours of useful practice. Since they offer instant feedback in the form of correct answers, they facilitate learning and retention. In addition, taped grammar exercises can be used selectively. You can concentrate on the items that give you trouble and skip the ones you already know.

At more advanced levels, tapes can help improve your listening comprehension as well. If your school or college has a tape library that includes stories, plays, songs, speeches, lectures, radio broadcasts, and the like, practicing listening comprehension may be very entertaining.

Some learners find that speaking or singing along with tapes increases their fluency. Others have found that listening to tapes with soft music in the background reduces distractions and helps them remember better. You may wish to experiment with these ways of listening to taped material as well.

One thing that tapes and recordings cannot help you develop is the ability to communicate with people in face-to-face situations. Gestures, expressions, moods, and settings are all absent from tapes. Only personal contact with native speakers can provide you with all the information you need to communicate effectively. However, with the advent of the videocassette, we can anticipate a time in the near future when audio-visual materials can be specially prepared for language courses.

REFERENCE GRAMMARS

Sometimes your basic text does not provide all the grammar information you need. You may therefore wish to supplement it with a reference grammar. Since there are many foreign-language reference grammars on the market, you should ask your teacher to recommend one that is appropriate to your level or objectives.

A reference grammar is organized by topic, so that all information on nouns, for instance, is in one place. This makes it easier to look up things. In fact, you may find your reference grammar easier to use than your textbook if you have a question about a grammar point.

Sometimes you may need more extensive explanations of the structures presented in your textbook. A reference grammar will usually provide the additional details you need. Periodically, you may find it useful to examine your reference grammar's more extended tables of declensions and conjugations to check how much you have learned. For advanced language students, a reference grammar may provide examples of complex grammar constructions not included in basic texts. At advanced levels, a reference grammar may be the only useful source of grammar information.

Verb guides are easy-to-use reference books that provide information about verb conjugations, usage, and the like. In addition, monolingual dictionaries furnish information about declensions, conjugations, and usage.

THE WIDER WORLD

Exposure to a language in a natural setting is a very important aspect of learning. In fact, rarely, if ever, do adults learn a language well if they do not practice it informally. As a serious language student, you should seek out as many opportunities as possible to observe how your new language is used and practice your own skills.

In Strategy 4, we described ways in which you can practice your language skills. Below we will list some of the places where you can expect to find or learn about opportunities to use your skills.

OPPORTUNITIES FOR CONVERSATION

1. Join a language club in your school or community.

2. Join the international club in your school or community.

3. Go to a language camp where the language is used.

4. Host an international student for dinner, or for an entire academic period.

5. Host international visitors who may wish to see how people in your country typically live.

6. Volunteer time in a retirement home or hospital where senior citizens or patients speak the language you want to learn.

7. Visit an ethnic church or community center and join in the social activities.

8. Visit an ethnic restaurant and use your foreign language to order food and talk to people.

9. Visit an ethnic store and use your foreign language while shopping.

10. Try to make friends with at least one person from a country where your new language is spoken.

OPPORTUNITIES TO LISTEN

1. Listen to community language broadcasts on the radio.

2. Listen to short-wave radio for Voice of America programs or broadcasts from countries where your new language is used.

3. Attend lectures in the language you are studying at your local university or cultural center.

4. Go to foreign-language movies.

5. Listen to songs in your new language.

6. Watch foreign-language television.

7. Contact the consulates of countries where your new language is spoken to learn about the activities they sponsor.

OPPORTUNITIES TO READ

Read ethnic or national newspapers, magazines, and books on subjects that interest you.

OPPORTUNITIES TO WRITE

1. Keep a diary in your new language.

2. Find a pen pal by writing to a newspaper in a country where your new language is spoken, a cultural attaché, or a pen pal service.

SELECTING THE LANGUAGE COURSE THAT'S RIGHT FOR YOU

One of the most important steps towards success in foreign-language learning is selecting the course of study that's right for you. Here are some things to consider in making your decision.

1. If you know your objectives for studying another language, be sure that the course you choose will help you attain them. For instance, if your objective is to learn to speak the language, make sure that the course you take emphasizes that skill. If, on the other hand, you want to learn to read materials in your field of specialization, avoid a course that stresses conversation.

2. When shopping for a language course, take into account how soon you need to reach your goal. For instance, if you must learn to speak a language within one year, look for an intensive program that will give you many hours of practice in a short period of time.

3. If you need outside motivation to keep studying, look for a standard classroom language course. If, however, you enjoy working steadily on your own and do not need the motivation provided by a teacher and regularly scheduled class meetings, consider a self-study or individualized course. Such programs allow you to set your own pace and require only periodic visits for testing rather than regular attendance. While independent study permits you to decide how much, when, and how you will learn, it also requires you to accept full responsibility for your learning. If you are prepared to take on such responsibility, a self-instructional course might be a good idea, particularly if learning to read and understand is more important to you than learning to speak.

4. Consider the amount of experience you have in learning other languages. If you are a very inexperienced language learner, you may lack the learning skills necessary for a self-instructional course. If, on the other hand, you are an experienced language learner, a self-instructional or individualized program might be just right for you.

5. If you are interested in longterm study of a foreign language, find a program that offers courses at all levels of proficiency. This will ensure your smooth progress from level to level. Transferring from program to program has many disadvantages, including incompatibility of textbooks, methods, and amount of material covered. Institutions vary widely in their curricula for first-, second-, and third-year language courses. You can avoid much frustration by choosing a program that will meet your needs well into the future.

6. Another language can be learned in a variety of settings, including the ideal combination of formal classroom instruction and informal exposure to the language in its natural setting. It is therefore important that you consider the amount of practice a particular program offers outside the classroom. For instance, some intensive summer programs, such as those at Middlebury College in Vermont, require that students sign a pledge not to use English either inside or outside of the classroom. The students reside in foreign-language dormitories (Russian house, French house, Spanish house, etc.) where they speak the language among themselves and with the resident manager. This arrangement provides countless hours of language practice in everyday situations.

7. It is becoming increasingly possible for American students to study foreign languages abroad. You may therefore want to consider the possibility of studying abroad through a university-sponsored program, an exchange program, or some other arrangement. At the intermediate and advanced levels, this may be the best way to improve language skills.

When looking into a language course in a foreign country, consider its duration; some courses are so short that you could not possibly acquire much proficiency. Thus, a three-week language-study plus sightseeing trip to France may be great fun and a good way to learn about France and the French people, but it will probably not greatly improve your knowledge or use of the French language.

8. Last, but not least, be realistic about the amount of time you can spend on studying a foreign language. Language courses are usually very demanding, so be sure that you can devote enough time to make the course worthwhile.

LOCATING THE RIGHT LANGUAGE COURSE

Foreign languages are widely taught. In every large metropolitan area in the United States, as well as in most medium-sized and small cities, you can find instruction in at least several foreign languages. Of course, the so-called commonly taught languages, such as French, Spanish, and German, are prevalent. Finding courses in the more exotic languages may be more difficult, however, and in such cases, you may wish to consider some form of self-instruction. The National Association of Self-Instructional Language Programs (NASILP) has a large network of institutions that offer self-study programs in many uncommonly taught languages. Your local librarian should know how to contact this organization. In addition, Ohio State University has produced individualized-study materials for six languages—French, Spanish, German, Russian, Latin, and Arabic. These materials require regular testing, however, and unless you can arrange for someone to administer the tests, you will find the programs somewhat difficult to tackle.

Here is a list of institutions that might offer language courses in your vicinity:

1. county departments of education
2. community colleges
3. universities
4. university extension programs
5. university alumni programs
6. high schools
7. ethnic organizations, including churches and clubs
8. commercial language schools, such as Berlitz
9. foreign government-sponsored organizations, such as *Alliance Francaise*
10. public and educational television stations

There is no question that you can learn a foreign or second language because you have already learned your native language. You have a great deal of knowledge and skills which you can bring to bear on this new task. In this book, we call your attention to the kinds of knowledge you need to recognize and some skills you should develop in order to master a new language. Further, you need to know how to use the many kinds of aids which are available in your community which can greatly contribute to your progress. With well-developed knowledge and skills, the task of language learning can be a rewarding challenge. This book should make the challenge a lot more comprehensible and manageable. For some it will become an interesting game. We hope that you will find it so.

About the Authors

Joan Rubin, sociolinguist and specialist in English language teaching, has her doctorate in anthropology. She has achieved near-native competency in several languages and considers herself a "good language learner." After receiving university training in teaching English as a second language, she taught English in Brazil and at Georgetown University. Dr. Rubin also has trained Peace Corps volunteers in language-teaching theory and methodology. For the past several years, she has been doing research on the learning strategies of "good language learners," and her work has inspired further exploration of this subject area by others. Dr. Rubin has also undertaken innovative research on sources of miscommunication across languages and cultures.

Irene Thompson, psycholinguist and professor of Russian, has been actively investigating the process of language learning for a very long time. Proficient in several languages in addition to English and to her mother tongue, Russian, Mrs. Thompson is currently director of the Russian language program at the State Department's Foreign Service Institute. Prior to this, she taught Russian over a period of some 15 years at George Washington University as well as at other universities. Consistent with her interest in the language learning process, she has also taught a number of courses in language-teaching methodology. Mrs. Thompson is the author of a number of articles on aspects of learning Russian as a foreign language.